THE APPRENTICE MINDSET

Hi George,
Perhaps your twins will find
this book useful when they
get older.
                    warm regards,
                        katanya

THE APPRENTICE MINDSET

KEYS FOR YOUR PROFESSIONAL JOURNEY

KATARVIA TAYLOR

NEW DEGREE PRESS

THE APPRENTICE MINDSET
Keys for Your Professional Journey

ISBN   979-8-88504-106-5 *Paperback*
         979-8-88504-735-7 *Kindle Ebook*
         979-8-88504-214-7 *Ebook*

To my parents, Earle and Betty

Contents

———

Author's Note

——

What *is* an apprentice mindset? How can it help you navigate and accelerate your professional career?

The Apprentice Mindset gives early career advice that is distilled from experience, observation, and research. It offers examples of successful starting-out strategies and tells the stories of those who succeeded brilliantly as a result of choices and decisions they made when they were new to a job. It explains why their careers became stellar and how they learned from their masters and went on to make their singular mark on history. *The Apprentice Mindset* makes clear how different choices of priorities can play out later in dramatically different ways, and how decisions and attitudes at the beginning of one's career or during a transition can make the difference between distinguishing oneself as one matures professionally...or remaining a tiny cog.

You can read the chapters in order, or you can select the keys and stories that most interest you and seem most applicable to the answers you are looking for. Let this book speak to you, and enjoy the journey!

Chapter 1: What Is an Apprenticeship? An apprenticeship is a transactional relationship whereby a master trains an apprentice in his/her craft under a contractual agreement that defines the conditions and terms of the working relationship.

Chapter 2: Observe to Grow—Shun the Must-Impress Mindset and Embrace the Apprentice Mindset. The transition from college to workforce or from one career to another is an exciting time. You may feel tempted or pressured to impress from the minute you walk through the door—but resist the urge. Instead of adopting a must-impress mindset, which is single-mindedly focused on impressing the higher-ups, take on an apprentice's mindset. Be curious, observe, and learn; focus on reproducing the excellence you observe. Prioritize observational learning. Watch the master. Soak up the behaviors, attitudes, and skills they are modeling—then imitate and improve on them to achieve mastery.

Chapter 3: Take Advantage of Tacit Knowledge: Learn "Know-How" from the Masters. Tacit knowledge is the type of knowledge, skills, ideas, and experiences that are not easily transmissible. During an apprenticeship, you will be able to benefit from the master's "know-how" knowledge (practical knowledge on how to do something), which differs from explicit or "know-what" knowledge (facts).

Chapter 4: To Ape or Not to Ape? Imitate, Don't Emulate...in the Beginning. At the beginning of your career, or during a transition, some skills are like a black box whose inner workings are hard to discern and understand. These are the complex skills you learn by imitating masters in precise detail. As counterintuitive as it may seem, imitating masters—copying their exact actions—will help you grasp skills more quickly and give you a deeper and more rapid cognitive understanding of the environment. At the outset, you do not want to emulate results, you want to imitate processes. In that way, you will gain access to a level of understanding that is revealed only when you go through the actions. This chapter makes clear how imitation allows for the kind of deep cultural learning that leads to mastery: You do not just learn *from* others, you learn *through* them.

Chapter 5: Prioritize the "Who" over the What and Where. When you are assessing job options, among your top three considerations should be who you will be working with. Salary, titles, and prestigious company names are seductive and of course important; in the long run, however, they will not accelerate skill acquisition the way working with a master does. The relationship with the master is likely to gain the apprentice access to people and rooms where they will be able to observe plans and decisions being made and pick up on the skills needed to move up to the next level.

Chapter 6: Develop Soft Skills: Build the Interpersonal Skills and Personal Traits Needed to Succeed. Soft skills are difficult to learn in a classroom. Watching, imitating, and tacit learning will teach you how to influence others and think strategically. Adopting an apprentice mindset that is predicated on learning from the most successful master will teach you drive, resilience, versatility, and the ability to solve complex problems.

Chapter 7: Welcome and Seek Out Tough Feedback. Feedback is a gift. It gives you insight into how you are perceived and where you need more development or course-correction. Receiving tough feedback can be hard on the ego, but seeking it out proactively will allow you to accelerate your professional development. When you get it, you should reflect and act on it.

Chapter 8: Read the Air: Learn the Unspoken and Unwritten Rules. All societies, communities, and cultures have unspoken and unwritten rules. No one will tell you what they are because they are embedded in the environment and in the social matrix, and thus are invisible and unarticulated. As a newcomer, you must look for them, learn them, and adopt them, and the best way to do this is by observing and imitating the people who are masters of your new domain.

Chapter 9: Learn Fast, Work Hard, and Deliver Results. An apprenticeship is not only about learning—you have to deliver quality and, ideally, excellence. Work hard to meet high expectations and, in time, you will achieve mastery and enter the guild of masters.

Chapter 10: Let's Get Practical—Starting, Managing, and Ending an Apprenticeship. Apprenticeships are finite and transactional; they will have a beginning and an end. When starting, choose a master to observe and imitate. Manage and nurture the relationship with this admired and respected person. Observe the master's high expectation of themselves and meet their high expectations of you. Put in the hard work (and the long hours). Take on assignments that stretch and challenge you. When it is time to move on, express sincere gratitude. Don't burn bridges; lay the groundwork for on-going relationships. When you have achieved mastery, set out on your own. When the opportunity arises, help someone in the way others have helped you.

PART I

Introduction

—

Apprenticeship is a proven model for developing a skilled workforce.

EUGENE SCALIA

One cold winter afternoon in 2017, I was working with my boss from her home office in Reston, Virginia. Rosa was sitting at her massive wooden desk reading briefing material, and I sat comfortably on a Persian rug, my legs folded under me and my back against the legs of a plush red guest chair. My laptop was on the coffee table in front of me, as was a second monitor, a notebook, two pens, three cell phones, and a bottle of water. I was multitasking. Between answering sporadic questions on the content of the briefing material, I was responding to e-mails and WhatsApp messages while keeping a watchful eye on the clock: A conference call was going to start in a few minutes.

Three minutes before call time, I dialed us into the teleconference, muted the phone, and waited for the host, someone who was looking to conduct business with Rosa in Africa. It was a routine call, and I knew the drill: Rosa would listen, assess if something was there, and if yes, I would operationalize it.

At that point, I had been working with The Whitaker Group (TWG) for two years. TWG is a leading transaction advisory and project development company doing business in Africa, with offices in Washington, DC, and Accra, Ghana. My role as senior director for international projects and operations was like that of chief of staff—the equivalent of making sure the trains ran on time. I had embraced the challenge to support Rosa Whitaker, TWG's founder and CEO, the first-ever US assistant trade representative for Africa, and one of the key architects of the African Growth and Opportunity Act (AGOA), the United States' key trade policy with Africa. I was grateful for the opportunity to work closely with, and learn from, a successful visionary. I followed Rosa around the world, shuttling between my home in DC, a company apartment in Ghana, and countries in East and West Africa, China, and the Middle East. Whenever a client needed Rosa, I packed my suitcase.

When the person on the other end of the phone clicked in, Rosa straightened her body, picked up the phone (even though it was on speaker), smiled (even though it was not a video call), and alerted her counterpart I was in the room with her. Rosa would be depending on my notes after the call, so I got up from the floor, picked up my notebook and pen, sat in the guest chair, and leaned in.

I accompanied Rosa on 90 percent of her calls and meetings. By now I had perfected a system for taking notes that captured the gist of the call and the action points. After two years, I knew what to write down and what to store in my head.

The call that day was different. While I thought the fancy fireplace with the gas crystals added a nice touch, coupled with the central heating, the room was too toasty for me. I locked my eyes on Rosa's face, ready to read any signals she would communicate. As I focused in, I began to feel strange, as if I was having an out of body experience. I was suddenly watching my brain coordinate my faculties, dictating which body parts would do what during the call. I felt my hand being tasked with capturing the content of the call. My fingers appeared to have developed a brain of their own, as if they were being assigned to take notes without assistance from my ears. My eyes and ears, meanwhile, had been given the role of capturing the form of the call—their job was to listen and watch for what was said and not said, and how it was communicated.

The call was a masterful *pas de deux*. The caller began by thanking Rosa for her time and was effusively appreciative of the mutual connection that had brought them together. Both Rosa and the caller said positive things about the individual; they then found a handful of people they had in common in their respective networks and reminisced briefly about the "good ol' days." The call then shifted to the topic at hand, and the caller launched seamlessly into his elevator pitch. Rosa listened intently and scribbled a few things in her notebook; she then shifted in her seat and began her solo piece. She asked insightful questions, gave some strategic advice (without revealing too much), and then offered to connect the caller with other people in her network with whom there would be greater potential for a mutually beneficial relationship.

After she hung up, she explained to me there had been no alignment or synergy with TWG's business model. I sent a note to her assistant, asking her to remind Rosa to make the connection she had promised. Rosa then went on to "seize a teachable moment" (as my mother would have described it), explaining why her years of experience working in Africa had made her give the advice she had given.

For me, however, that was not the greatest lesson of the call. Reflecting on what I had just witnessed, I experienced a sort of epiphany. I realized there were patterns and algorithms to how everything happened. These calls and meetings had a certain standard choreography, with slight variations appropriate to the situation and context. Up until this point in my tenure with the company, I had been focused on getting smarter and more efficient at operationalizing projects in Africa and facilitating whatever endeavor Rosa decided to take on, but I had not been consciously tuned into what was really happening at the macro level.

I had been spending seven to eight hours a day with Rosa in her office, sitting in on calls and meetings and drafting client e-mails and reports. While traveling, we would spend 97 percent of our waking hours together, preparing for and attending meetings, working out in the hotel gym, and eating. I had the privilege of seeing how a seasoned entrepreneur, diplomat, and former WTO trade negotiator got things done. She allowed me behind the curtain to observe and assist her in doing what she did. The days and nights were tough, but the work was rewarding, and I learned a great deal. She taught me the importance of diplomacy, tone, and atmospherics of doing business in Africa.

In 2017, Deloitte published an article on the five ways to nurture developing leaders in an ecosystem for growth. The article's authors noted the best way to nurture talent and leadership is not by sending the individual to courses and training seminars; rather, it is by creating an environment in which learning can happen. The way to create that environment, they asserted, is to pair the individual with people from whom they can learn. The article states,

> *The organizations with the strongest results in terms of financial and business outcomes were those that develop leaders by connecting them with other leaders and providing continuing opportunities for emerging and growing leaders to exchange information, knowledge, and new ideas about the company identity and leadership profile (Derler, Abbatiello, and Garr, 2017).*

The article goes on to say:

> *Out of 111 potential practices we tested in our survey, the data revealed more than a dozen that were strongly correlated to business and leadership outcomes. Looking closer at these practices, we found five of these critical practices share one underlying theme: leaders tend to learn best with other leaders and from other leaders (Derler, Abbatiello, and Garr, 2017).*

What they are describing is, in effect, an apprenticeship—the pairing of an experienced leader (a master) with a potential leader (an apprentice).

I decided to write this book because I have had the opportunity to observe highly skilled individuals like Rosa in action. Intrigued by their ability to solve tough problems with mind-blowing innovation and creativity, I felt impelled to dig deeper and ask them to share with me the key to their success. In most cases, there was no secret sauce; they had simply developed and honed their skills by working closely with experts and had learned in the trenches. Most had had an apprenticeship with an expert in their field, or they had possessed the mindset of an apprentice in that they had sought out masters in their field and submitted themselves in order to learn, grow, and develop their own proficiency.

Formalized education is an option; however, the arts and vocational fields still use apprenticeships as the primary method for passing on knowledge. This is very much apparent in the field of classical music, where achieving greatness is not just a function of over ten thousand hours of deliberate practice to develop one's skill; the required X factor is the honing of one's craft under the tutelage of a master.

In the following pages, I will share the stories of people who engaged in apprenticeships in order to accelerate skill acquisition and achieve mastery and success.

- In Part 1, I define what an apprenticeship is and how it is different from other developmental relationships such as internships, mentorships, and advisory relationships.

I outline its benefits, arguing an apprenticeship is a powerful relationship.

- In Part 2, I share stories of master/apprentice pairs and the results of my research into what made the relationship, and the apprentice, a success.

- Part 3 is about application. In that section, I look at how apprenticeships start and end, and I share tips on managing masters.

This book is for students, recent graduates, young professionals, and those making a career change. It is also for people who consider themselves to be lifelong learners.

My hope is that this book inspires an appreciation for the masters among us and the processes by which mastery is achieved. I hope you are encouraged and motivated by the stories of the masters who pulled greatness out of their apprentices by taking them along for the ride and by the apprentices who were brave enough to follow and keep up with the masters, eventually achieving mastery and stratospheric success.

CHAPTER 1

What Is an Apprenticeship?

———

apprentice (n.)

"one bound by legal agreement to an employer to learn a craft or trade," c. 1300, from Old French *aprentiz* "someone learning"

apprentice (adj.)

"unskilled, inexperienced," from *aprendre* "to learn; to teach" (Modern French *apprendre*), contracted from Latin *apprehendere* "take hold of, grasp" mentally or physically, in Medieval Latin "to learn"

apprentice (v.)

"to bind to a master for instruction in his craft," 1630s

ONLINE ETYMOLOGY DICTIONARY

In 1472, Andrea del Verrocchio completed his famous painting, *The Baptism of Christ*, an altarpiece commissioned by the monks of the San Salvi church near Florence, Italy, and now in Florence's Uffizi Gallery. Besides being considered a great work of fifteenth-century Renaissance art, one of the painting's points of note is that Leonardo da Vinci, who was Verrocchio's apprentice at the time, assisted the master painter, sculptor, and goldsmith on the work. Da Vinci distinguished himself by painting the angel on the left, which is noted for the articulated pose of its body and the realistic draping of the angel's light-blue robes.

Leonardo da Vinci was born in 1452. He is one of history's indisputable geniuses, demonstrating artistic talent at an early age. His father was notary to many of Florence's elite and was able to apprentice his son to Verrocchio, who had a renowned workshop.

During his seven-year apprenticeship in Verrocchio's atelier, da Vinci received diverse and in-depth training in drafting, woodwork, drawing, painting, and sculpting, all of which dovetailed well with his dual interest in art and science.

The same year *The Baptism of Christ* was completed, da Vinci qualified as a master in the Guild of Saint Luke, of which Verrocchio was also a member. With this, he had formally completed his apprenticeship; however, he decided to remain with Verrocchio—who was regarded as a remarkable teacher and master—for a further five years.

In 2019, Andrew Butterfield, a curator of the Smithsonian Museum, described Verrocchio's workshop as a laboratory for the art of the High Renaissance; it was a place where "in a relatively small space, you had all these budding geniuses." He described Verrocchio as a visionary "[with a] restless imagination and relentless drive to experiment and improve on what he or anyone else had done before. But he was like the maestro of the orchestra who could bring together many talents and draw forth the best from them" (Solly, 2019).

Italian poet Ugolino Verino, paying tribute to Verrocchio after his death in 1488, noted, "Whatever painters have that is good, they drank from Verrocchio's spring" (National Gallery of Art). He thus paid homage to the master of a workshop that had trained some of the greatest painters of all time, including, besides da Vinci, Lorenzo di Credi and Pietro Perugino, who would become Raphael's teacher.

Verrocchio, born Andrea di Michele di Francesco de' Cioni, was born in Florence in 1435. He apprenticed with goldsmith Giuliano Verrocchio, from whom he took his new surname. Verrocchio later went on to work as a sculptor, metalworker, and painter and was employed by Florence's powerful Medici family, who were devoted patrons of the arts and humanities and who inspired the flourishing of the Italian Renaissance. An excellent sculptor, Verrocchio designed a bronze statue of David for the Medicis; it is considered one of the greatest sculptures of all time and was meant to represent Florence's rise to power.

While da Vinci achieved far more success and acclaim than did his master, Verrocchio is credited with having originated the twisting pose, or *figura serpentinata*, and the study of contrasting expressions—two techniques that da Vinci perfected (The National Gallery).

Leonardo da Vinci possessed a singular talent, a unique ability to translate what he observed and thought onto paper and into stone and metal. His skill, creativity, and curiosity were unique; however, it must be remembered that his genius was incubated and forged in Verrocchio's workshop.

Talent is developed and honed under the guidance of a master—therein lies the power of the master-apprentice relationship.

DEFINING APPRENTICESHIPS

TRADITIONALLY...

As early as the eighteenth century BCE, apprenticeships have been formalized as a means of acquiring and passing on skills and expertise. The Code of Hammurabi of Babylon, which dates from that time, required artisans to teach their crafts to the next generation. In Rome and other ancient societies, many craftsmen were slaves, but, in the later years of the Roman Empire, craftsmen began to organize into independent collegia, which were formed to uphold the standards of their trades (Britannica). Over the centuries and in a quite similar format around the world, parents arranged for their children to apprentice in the workshop of a master craftsman in order to gain a skill and thereby a means of sustaining themselves in the world.

- In medieval Europe, parents enrolled and paid for their male children to participate in formal apprenticeships whereby they lived with a master and learned the craft. The average length of an apprenticeship was five to seven years, during which the master would provide education on the craft as well as moral and cultural education. Apprentices received no compensation other than their food, clothing, and lodging. At the end of the apprenticeship period, graduates would show their mastery by producing a "masterpiece" that reflected the culmination of the skills they had learned. After completion of an apprenticeship, it was only after paying for the privilege that the designation of "master" could be used. Qualified apprentices who could not afford to pay for the title or open their own workshops would become "journeymen" who traveled and worked with a master wherever they could. Those who became masters and opened their own workshops joined "guilds," which served as regulatory organizations for the master tradesmen.

- In West Africa, parents would place their children with masters to whom they delegated some of their parental authority. The master would be responsible for training, educating, and imparting the culture of the field to the apprentice. The apprenticeship occurred over four phases: (1) observing the master and internalizing their behavior; (2) learning the names and use of instruments and doing simple and repetitive tasks; (3) taking on complex tasks, completing full projects, and beginning to negotiate with customers; and (4) completing the apprenticeship and being released by the master (Walther and Filipiak, 2008). In some African countries—depending on the trade—the length of the apprenticeship was fixed, while in other countries, the master determined its length (International Labour Organization, 2020). The end of the apprenticeship was celebrated with a release ceremony, confirming the apprentice was now a full professional (Walther and Filipiak, 2008). Often regarding the apprentice as a family member to whom they had a moral obligation, a master would assist their apprentice in setting up their own business.

- In China, apprenticeships included on-the-job training and study of the professional context and milieu. Apprenticeships were divided into three stages: (1) education, where the apprentice would observe the master and learn the necessary skills; (2) training, during which novices learned and honed the spirit of craftsmanship, which was based on precision, patience, and perfection; and (3) empowerment, where the master would isolate the apprentice to empower them with autonomy and provide space for creativity. Masters were seen as parental figures, responsible for encouraging the apprentice and teaching them through their own modeling of good behavior and conduct. Apprentices were expected to work hard and obey their master, and the best apprentice would be selected by the master to be their successor (Zhang and Cerdin, 2020).

IN ITS MODERN FORM

Apprenticeships today are mostly organized and regulated by governments and businesses in order to ensure companies can develop a pipeline of skilled workers. Across the globe, countries tend to focus on vocational and technological training to ensure their citizens have the skills necessary to support a competitive economy.

- In the United Kingdom, the government serves as a clearinghouse for connecting apprentices looking for hands-on training with businesses who are looking to grow and develop talent. To support these programs, all UK employers that make over three million pounds a year are required to pay an apprenticeship levy of 0.5 percent.

- Germany's apprenticeship program is based on its dual training system whereby vocational education and vocational work are combined. Apprentices attend a technical college to learn theory and learn the practical skills on the job site. Apprenticeships typically last two to three-and-a-half years (Bundesagentur für Arbeit).

- In the United States, an individual may enter a Registered Apprenticeship Program (RAP), which has been validated by the US Department of Labor or by a State Apprenticeship Agency. An Industry-Recognized Apprenticeship Program (IRAP), much like a RAP, includes a paid-work component and an educational component and results in an industry-recognized credential. IRAPs are developed or delivered by entities such as trade and industry groups, corporations, and non-profits (Apprenticeship.Gov). Such programs include connecting employers with apprentices.

- In China, the government launched its modern apprenticeship program in line with its five-year strategic plan. The government plays a central role by coordinating and monitoring participating schools and businesses. A formal agreement between the school and the company and between the master and the apprentice describes the responsibilities, duties, learning objectives, salary, working hours, conditions, and liabilities (Zhang and Cerdin, 2020). Programs are between one and three years. Government subsidies incentivize companies to participate in apprenticeship programs (*Global Times*, 2021).

A WORKING DEFINITION

An apprenticeship, for the purpose of this book, is an arrangement whereby a master trains an apprentice in his/her craft under a contractual agreement that defines the conditions and terms of the working relationship.

PHASES

Robert Greene, author of the *New York Times* bestseller *Mastery,* defines the phases of an apprenticeship as: deep observation, skills acquisition, and experimentation.

- *Deep Observation—Passive Mode*: During this phase, apprentices should observe the master performing a particular skill. According to Greene, "When you enter a new environment, you will need to observe the world, the players, and the environment. During this phase, you want to learn as much as you can." He notes further, "You will become accustomed to observing first, basing your ideas and theories on what you have seen with your eyes, and then analyzing what you find" (Greene, 2012).

- **Skills Acquisition—Practice Mode**: This is an approximation phase wherein the apprentice learns to imitate the master's actions and compare results. Greene notes during the skills acquisition phase, learning takes place thanks to the power of mirror neurons in the brain. Apprentices gain skill by watching and imitating others and then repeating the action over and over. In the process, they are also able to observe themselves and receive feedback from others. According to Greene, a key aspect of this phase is…

> …when you practice and develop any skill you transform yourself (…). You reveal to yourself new capabilities that were previously latent, that are exposed as you progress. You develop emotionally. (…) Although it might seem that the time necessary to master the requisite skills and attain a level of expertise would depend on the field and your own talent level, those who have researched the subject repeatedly come up with the number of ten thousand hours. Although the number of hours might seem high, it generally adds up to seven to ten years of sustained, solid practice— roughly the period of a traditional apprenticeship. In other words, concentrated practice over time cannot fail, but produce results (Greene, 2012).

- **Experimentation—Active Mode**: During this phase of the apprenticeship, apprentices should take on more responsibility and start to practice their skills in the real world. At this point, they begin to engage in self-directed learning—attempting to perform tasks they understand well in real time within real society. They then start to apply what they have learned to other relevant domains. Greene notes during this phase, apprentices test their character; they move past their fears and begin to acquire a taste for what it feels like to perform work under scrutiny. The apprenticeship is over when the apprentice feels they have nothing left to learn in the environment. At that point, it is time to either start an apprenticeship elsewhere to further expand their skill base, or move into mastery via the creation of a masterpiece.

APPRENTICESHIPS VS. OTHER DEVELOPMENTAL RELATIONSHIPS

Based on the definition of an apprenticeship as a process by which a beginner acquires skills and competencies from an expert, how does it differ from other growth and development relationships such as internships, mentorships, advisorships, and sponsorships?

The difference can be summed up in four words: formality, nature, duration, and focus.

- *Formality*. An apprenticeship is structured and happens in a formal environment. The relationship between the master and the apprentice is a clearly hierarchical structure, whereby the apprentice is subordinate to the master and the master has a certain level of decision-making power over the apprentice's career.

- *Nature*. The apprentice understands they are supposed to be learning from, not trying to compete with, the master. The master understands while the apprentice will add value to the organization or business, they are primarily trying to build expertise and competencies. In other words, it is a highly transactional relationship: the apprentice wants to gain skills, while the master makes use of relatively inexpensive labor and benefits from harnessing potential talent for the organization during the apprentice's tenure.

- **Duration.** An apprenticeship takes place over a defined period of time. The goal is for the apprentice to build skills toward achieving mastery and then move on.

- **Focus.** In an apprenticeship, the *who* is more important than the *what* and the *where*; that is, the skillset of the master is much more important than the prestige of the organization. Only one criterion applies: If the person is skilled, they can assume the role of a master. It is a transactional relationship where the passing on of competencies and skills is the main objective.

Types of Developmental Relationships

Relationship	Formality	Nature	Time commit-ment	Duration	Focus	Parties
Apprentice-ship	Formal/ structured	Transactional	Full time or nearly full time	Defined/finite	Market-ready skills and competencies	Master and apprentice
Internship	Formal/ structured	Transactional and relational	Full time or part-time	Defined/finite	Résumé-building	Company and intern
Mentorship	Informal and formal	Relational	A few hours per week or month	Undefined/ open-ended	Personal or professional growth	Mentor and protégé
Advisorship	Informal	Transactional and relational	Only as needed	Undefined/ open-ended	Discrete advice	Advisor and advisee
Sponsorship	Formal and informal	Transactional and relational	Only as needed	Undefined/ open-ended	Promotions	Sponsor and candidate

- **Internships** are the little first cousins to apprenticeships. Like apprenticeships, internships tend to have a finite timeline and, from the outset, the intern knows the start and end dates of the relationship. I like to call internships the "wild wild West of career development." In an internship, the *what* and the *where* tend to take precedence, as the relationship in a lot of cases is between the company and the intern and does not necessarily involve a particular person in the company. While the spirit behind internships (paid and unpaid) is to provide an opportunity for the inexperienced to learn and gain real-world skills, they are sometimes regarded as résumé builders, wherein students can sometimes be overly focused on snagging a coveted summer job with a name-brand organization, even it means sitting in a basement stuffing envelopes. In far too many cases, interns are managed by inexperienced and overworked junior employees who view them as a dumping ground for administrative tasks that have become backlogged.

Carla Harris has one of the best explanations of the main professional relationships: mentorships, advisorships, and sponsorships. She is the senior client advisor at Morgan Stanley; she was vice chair of wealth management and, from 2005 to 2014, was chair of the Morgan Stanley Foundation. She was appointed by President Barack Obama to chair the National Women's Business Council and is the author of *Expect to Win* (Morgan Stanley, n.d.). Carla encourages readers to build their personal boards of directors to manage their careers.

- **Mentorships**. Unlike apprenticeships, the relationship between the mentor and mentee is personal and not merely transactional. Carla Harris notes,

> *So many people make the mistake of choosing a mentor only because they respect them professionally or because they are senior in an organization. These are, of course, very important criteria. However, if they don't really know you as a person and have some sense of who you are as a professional, they cannot be an effective mentor to you (...) because they don't really know you: your strengths, your weaknesses, your background, or the details of your career aspirations. An effective mentor will give you advice that is in context with all of these things and more. Your relationship with your mentor and the advice they give should be very specific to who you are and to the environment you work in (Harris, 2009).*

This is the exact opposite of an apprenticeship–master relationship, where the primary criterion for finding a master is their level of expertise. It does not matter if the master is nice, warm, or gentle.

- **Advisorships**. Harris notes advisors are knowledgeable, helpful people to whom the advisee can turn for what she refers to as "discrete advice," that is, advice that "pertain[s] to an isolated question you may have about some issue or challenge as opposed to advice and counsel that pertains to your career progression" (Harris, 2009). The advisor can show you "how" to do something. Like that of apprentice–master, a key driver around this relationship is the expertise of the advisor; however, in the case of advisor–advisee, interaction only occurs when answers are needed to discrete questions, and the advisee generally does not have sustained access to the advisor.

- **Sponsorship.** Carla defines a sponsor as someone who is willing to spend political and social capital on their candidate. As she puts it, sponsors "pound the table" behind closed doors on behalf of their candidates. Masters can eventually become sponsors, but the sponsorship relationship is only leveraged when needed; if there is no promotion or opportunity for career advancement, the sponsor need not take any active role.

A CASE FOR APPRENTICESHIPS

The apprenticeship relationship is the only professional developmental relationship where there is a sustained and constant opportunity to grow and receive feedback.

A key characteristic of apprenticeships is their one-sidedness, which is to say the apprentice does most of the work. The master is required to merely show up and give feedback to the apprentice as to where they are doing well and where they need to course-correct. Not to be underestimated is the value gained by the apprentice in being allowed to enter the master's orbit. From there it is up to the apprentice to observe and reproduce the work of the master and eventually develop their own voice in the field.

The most important skill an apprentice can bring to the apprentice–master relationship is not—as one might expect—intelligence or charisma; rather, it is the ability to observe. "Observational learning" refers to the apprentice's ability to capture skills by watching the master intensely and picking up on the nuggets of wisdom and know-how that cannot be found in books; it is a type of learning that is organic and not instructional. While on occasion the master will actually instruct the apprentice, the vast majority of what the apprentice learns is gleaned from being around the master. Key to this is the apprentice's intentionality about watching. *That* is what is central to the *Apprentice Mindset.*

In the next chapter, we will explore observational learning and how simply paying attention can lead to mastery.

CHAPTER 2

Observe to Grow— Shun the Must-Impress Mindset and Embrace the Apprentice Mindset

———

Wisdom and understanding can only become the possession of individual men by traveling the old road of observation, attention, perseverance, and industry.

SAMUEL SMILES

In the early 1990s, someone asked fifth grader Maureen Magarity what she wanted to be when she grew up. She answered she wanted to be a basketball coach like her dad. Her father is Dave Magarity, former American women's basketball coach. Dave served as the head coach for Army West Point's women's basketball team from 2006 until his retirement from the sport in 2021.

College basketball is the Magarity family business. Dave's brother, both of his sisters, his son, his daughter, and his niece all played NCAA Division I basketball, the highest and most competitive level for intercollegiate sports.

Maureen grew up in Poughkeepsie, New York, where her father was head coach for the college men's basketball team at Marist College from 1986 to 2004. She lived and breathed basketball. She says it has always been a huge part of her life, and she caught the coaching bug at a very young age (Toland, 2021). She paid close attention to her father as he coached and prepared for games. She fondly reminisces about going to the gym to watch the Marist men's team practice, and anytime her father would review game film, she would pull up a chair and watch with him. As Dave recalls, "I remember her sitting there with me (…), I'd be doing a scout for an opponent, and she'd ask questions and I'd tell her, 'This is how you have to defend this, or whatever,' and she was pretty insightful, even at a young age" (ibid).

After graduating from high school, Maureen played at Boston College for one year before transferring to Marist in her hometown; there she was a lead scorer, team captain in her junior and senior years, and took the team to their first NCAA tournament in 2004. She then went on to begin her coaching career, landing a job that year as an assistant coach at Marist College. In 2006, Maureen joined her father's coaching team at Army West Point. The West Point team is part of the Patriot League, a collegiate athletic conference composed of private colleges and universities and the two US military academies (Army and Navy). For four years, Maureen served as assistant coach, watching her father and further developing her coaching skills and leadership ability. She credits working with Magarity Senior for shaping her as a leader and as a person, reflecting,

> I had the great opportunity to work for him for four years at West Point (...). Talking about leadership and working in an academy like West Point was just a tremendous experience for me and my development as a leader. (...) He's the type of head coach that gives a lot of responsibility to his assistants, and I think I really grew a lot as a young assistant coach (America East Conference, 2015).

In 2010, Maureen was offered the head coach position of the women's basketball team at the University of New Hampshire. During her ten successful years there, she built a strong program, and in 2017, she was named the Kay Yow National Coach of the Year. In 2020, she was recruited as head coach of Holy Cross, a member of the Patriot League, which Maureen had come to know very well during the four years assisting her father.

In early January 2021, with the Army and Holy Cross teams scheduled to play each other on the ninth, the media was all abuzz. It was not just a case of a head coach taking on a former assistant coach; more importantly, the Magarity–Magarity match-up made NCAA Division I history when they became the first father–daughter pair to face off on the court.

In advance of the game, sports outlets, morning talk shows, and bloggers all clamored to see how father and daughter felt about playing each other. Maureen told Fox News, "Playing against my dad, he's done such a great job throughout his coaching career (…) To survive coaching this long speaks volumes about my dad and what he's taught me. I'll try not to be emotional walking into that game" (Fox News, 2021). Her father told ESPN, "I came in thinking, 'I hope it's a good game, but I need to win'" (Voepel, 2021).

Holy Cross annihilated Army that weekend with a final score of eighty-six to forty. During the post-game interview, Dave admitted, "When I looked up and we were down by as many as thirty, I'm thinking to myself, 'What parallel universe am I living in? What is going on here?'" He added, "It was a tough game; my head's still spinning. We had been playing decent basketball, so I give them all the credit in the world. Their kids stepped up, they played great. There's no question, I'm proud of her as a father and the fact they were prepared" (Voepel, 2021).

Dave retired at the end of the 2020/2021 season, and Maureen went on to ride the wave at Holy Cross. As of this writing in 2022, Holy Cross is leading in the Patriot League for the 2021/2022 season.

Maureen successfully completed the phases of an apprenticeship before becoming the master who captivated and made history in American women's basketball. And it all started with observation.

Maureen's Passage through the phases of
an apprenticeship:

Phase	Description
Deep observation (passive mode)	Maureen observes her father coaching at Marist and reviews game film with him.
Skills acquisition (practice mode)	Maureen serves as assistant coach at Marist.
Experimentation (active mode)	Maureen receives the head coach position at New Hampshire University and then at Holy Cross, where she puts into practice years of observation and honed skills.

The young Maureen who spent hours watching her father, reviewing film with him, and working for him as his assistant coach made news headlines when she finally took on her dad. She had observed him for years, and when the time came, she showed she could implement everything she had learned over the decades, combining this learning with new skills and strategies that typically accompany firm foundations. The apprentice became a master.

Just as deep observation is the first phase of an apprenticeship, observation forms the base on which to build the foundation toward mastery. This is true in any sector, industry, or domain.

OBSERVATION AS THE FOUNDATION OF THE APPRENTICE MINDSET

In the 1970s, Dr. Jean Lave, a social anthropologist from the University of California, Berkeley, traveled to Monrovia, the capital city of Liberia in West Africa. There, she researched the apprenticeships of tailors working in a section of the city called Happy Corner. Observing the interactions between the apprentices and masters, Dr. Lave noted,

> *Apprenticeship in Happy Corner took about five years, and almost every apprentice became a master tailor. (...) The new apprentice lived with other apprentices in the shop. He learned first to sew by hand, to take care of the sewing machine, and to run small errands for his master. (...) Over the next several years, the apprentices learned to make all different kinds of clothes that were made in Happy Corner, and to do so with an economy of effort and a speed that was amazing to behold. Midway through the process, when they were skilled enough, the apprentices' work began to augment and supplement their masters' output and income, and they continued to work for them until they themselves became masters, ready to begin their own small, independent tailoring businesses. (...) The apprentices became masters when their masters had given them their blessing. (...) In theory, both master and apprentice were on trial for a period of time after an apprentice came to live with a master. (...) Tailors said that if a boy still could not sew buttons on trousers after three months, they would send him back to his parents—should it ever happen. But to be sent away for lack of aptitude would require an extraordinary exhibition of incompetence. (...) There were durable conflicts as well as common interests in apprentices' progress. Given the difference in power between apprentice and master, the most important concerned their long-term*

relations as patron and client and the temptation to
exploit apprentices in the shorter run. The master
could employ an apprentice as errand runner, house
servant, and farmhand, all of which would interfere
with the boy's opportunities to learn. Masters had
the formal responsibility to declare apprenticeship
complete, return the new master to his parents, and
convey legitimacy on his mastery through his bless-
ing (without which the tailors believed it would not
be possible to prosper in business). Timing mattered:
The master could hold on indefinitely to a skilled
apprentice as a source of cheap labor and would be
more likely to do so when demand for clothing was
high. In bad times, the apprentice might not want to
be pushed out on his own. Masters might be gener-
ous or tightfisted, and their apprentices thus either
more or less able to set up in business for themselves.
Apprentices thus had little leverage with which to
negotiate the end of their apprenticeships.

But there were limits on the masters as well: If a master badly
neglected his apprentice and didn't give him opportunities
to learn tailoring, the boy's family could intervene, and the
apprentice could leave this master and seek a new one. The
tailors gossiped about certain masters who exploited their
apprentices. And masters were, perhaps more compellingly,
dependent on the skills and industry of their apprentices for
their own livelihood. An advanced apprentice who left in
protest could not soon be replaced (Lave, 2011).

While Lave's description shows the process of mastery in a
vocational trade in Africa's informal economy, one can easily

see the similarities to corporate firms around the world. Each autumn, new hires enter businesses, perhaps with potential but zero-to-little knowledge of how things are done at their new workplace; they must work for, and with, masters to learn the job. In these companies—like in Liberia—these young hopefuls enter in cohorts and, over time, learn skills and gain abilities, while at the same time, increasingly adding value to their master's firm.

THE MUST-IMPRESS MINDSET VS. THE APPRENTICE MINDSET

For recent college graduates, the transition from college to the workforce is not a simple, straightforward shift from learning to producing; rather, it is a move from purely formal education to practical training. Robert Greene, in his book *Mastery*, notes, "After your formal education, you enter the most critical phase in your life—a second, practical education known as The Apprenticeship. Every time you change careers or acquire new skills, you reenter this phase of life" (Greene, 2012).

Too many entry-level employees, when they begin their first post-university job, make the mistake of bringing a "must-impress" mindset to the job. To them it makes sense: They had to impress college admissions officers to get into college, they had to impress professors to get that "A," and they had to impress the hiring committee to land this job. The system had worked so far. Teenagers and young adults learn they are constantly being assessed; as a consequence, they become skilled at the must-impress game. However, Greene cautions,

> *The greatest mistake you can make in the initial months of your apprenticeship is to imagine you have to get attention, impress people, and prove yourself. These thoughts will dominate your mind and close it off from the reality around you. Any positive attention you receive is deceptive; it is not based on your skills or anything real, and it will turn against you. Instead, you will want to acknowledge the reality and submit to it, muting your colors and keeping in the background as much as possible, remaining passive and giving yourself the space to observe. You will also want to drop any preconceptions you might have about this world you are entering. If you impress people in these first months, it should be because of the seriousness of your desire to learn, not because you are trying to rise to the top before you are ready (Greene, 2012).*

When you enter the real world of work, you must understand practical skill acquisition and true mastery are gained with an apprentice's mindset, that is, a mindset dominated by the kind of curiosity that is always observing, learning, and imitating.

OBSERVATIONAL LEARNING

If you have ever stuck your tongue out at a baby, you know babies learn by observing and imitating. It is how they make sense of the world.

In the 1960s, Canadian–American psychologist Albert Bandura carried out one of the most well-known experiments in the history of psychology, called the Bobo doll experiment. Bandura had children watch an adult behaving violently toward a Bobo doll, and then observed when the children were later left alone in the room to play with the doll, they began to imitate the aggression they had observed from the adults. This seminal experiment was taken as proof children learn and imitate behaviors they have observed in other people.

The results of the experiment led Bandura to develop social learning theory (later reconceptualized as social cognitive theory). Its core tenet was observational learning—the process by which someone learns by watching, memorizing, and then imitating the behaviors, attitudes, and emotional reactions of another person.

Bandura posits, "Most human behavior is learned observationally through modeling: From observing others, one forms an idea of how new behaviors are performed and on later occasions, this coded information serves as a guide for action" (Bandura, 1977).

He further notes there are four factors that influence observational learning: attention, retention, reproduction, and motivation and reinforcement.

In an apprenticeship, observational learning takes place through the modeling of behavior, attitudes, and skills by the master and observation by the apprentice (paying attention, retaining information). The apprentice imitates the master (reproduction), which then allows for the gaining of mastery and some modicum of success (motivation and reproduction).

- *Attention*: *One must be focused on the task.* This is a cognitive process of selectively concentrating on one thing and ignoring others, with paying attention to the model being a condition for learning. The ability to pay attention is affected by the individual's characteristics, including sensory capacities, arousal level, perception, and past reinforcement.

- *Retention*: *The behavior must be remembered.* You must remember what you paid attention to and internalize the information so you can recall it when encountering a similar situation. Remembering is a prerequisite for later imitation; included in this are symbolic coding and rehearsal, mental images, cognitive organization, and motor rehearsal.

- *Reproduction*: *The previously learned image or behavior must be reproduceable when required.* Practice improves your ability to perform. The person must have the capacity and skills to imitate the behavior. It makes no sense, for example, for an eight-year-old to try and dunk a basketball on an NBA rim after watching professional NBA players; indeed, it is physically impossible.

- *Motivation and Reinforcement*: *You must be motivated to imitate the behavior that has been modeled.* For our purposes, the motivation is mastery. The behavior must be useful or provide an incentive or reward for the learner. If the behavior is positively reinforced, the learner is motivated to repeat it.

While the Bobo doll experiment and social learning theory were developed in the context of how children learn, observational learning also very much applies to adult learning; it is how human beings learned before the formalization of education. We can therefore take the following maxim that *in an apprenticeship, observational learning takes place through the modeling of behavior, attitudes, and skills by the master and observation by the apprentice (paying attention, retaining information). The apprentice imitates the master (reproduction), which then allows for the gaining of mastery and some modicum of success (motivation and reproduction).*

Maureen Magarity observed her father's coaching for years, retained the concepts, and was able to reproduce it. The apprentice tailors in Liberia were required to observe how garments were sewn, retain what they observed, and then reproduce it. Both of these examples reflect the essence of how skills are acquired. In the following chapters, we will look at apprentice–master pairs and see how this cycle of attention, retention, and motivation and reinforcement plays out in real life.

PART II

CHAPTER 3

Take Advantage of Tacit Knowledge: Learn "Know-How" from the Masters

―――――

While tacit knowledge can be possessed by itself, explicit knowledge must rely on being tacitly understood and applied. Hence all knowledge is either tacit or rooted in tacit knowledge. A wholly explicit knowledge is unthinkable.

MICHAEL POLANYI

In 1946, thirty-year-old Bernard Greenhouse traveled from the United States to Prades, a small town in France near the border with Spain. He went there to train with seventy-year-old legendary Catalan cellist Pablo Casals. A few months prior, Greenhouse had asked Casals's protégé, Diran Alexanian, with whom Greenhouse had studied, to send a letter on his behalf to Casals, asking him to listen to him play his cello. Casals declined, explaining he was busy helping Spanish refugees who had fled the Franco regime and were seeking asylum in France.

Disappointed but undeterred, Greenhouse decided to reach out to Casals himself. Moved by Greenhouse's determination, Casals told him, "I'll listen to you play, but first donate one hundred dollars to the cause of the Spanish charities that are working with Spanish exiles in France" (Janof, 2016). Greenhouse accepted the terms, and Casals agreed to listen to him play.

When Greenhouse appeared at Casals's home, the master welcomed him and invited him to play for him; however, the pressure of playing for the renowned cellist weighed heavily on Greenhouse. Noticing he was uncontrollably and visibly shaking with nerves, Casals got up, left the room, and told Greenhouse to warm up. Twenty minutes later, wondering what was taking Casals so long to return, Greenhouse noticed him just outside the door of the room. Casals told him, "I wanted to hear how you play when you are not nervous." Touched by Casals's sensitivity, Greenhouse went on to spend the next forty-five minutes playing pieces the maestro requested. When he was done, Casals looked at him and said,

I believe what you need most of all is the association with a great artist because I believe in the apprentice system. It is not only the instrument, but it's the artist. You learn so much through personal association with the artist and I don't know who to send you to, so if you agree, stay for at least six months and take lessons several times a week; I'll teach you (*Janof, 2016*).

And so began Bernard Greenhouse's apprenticeship with Pablo Casals.

Pablo Casals was born in 1876 in El Vendrell, Catalonia. He first heard a cello played at the age of eleven and begged his father to get him one. At twelve, he innovated a new technique for playing the cello, and at thirteen, he found a copy of Bach's six *Cello Suites* and spent the following thirteen years practicing them every day; only then did he play them in public. An extremely disciplined and structured person, he lived by the maxim that "organization is essential to creative work." He was known to practice six to seven hours per day. His international career was quite notable; he performed for President Roosevelt and Queen Victoria and played in many major concert halls, including Carnegie Hall and the Crystal Palace in London. He was a political activist who openly opposed Francisco Franco's dictatorship in Spain. He received a Presidential Medal of Honor from President John F. Kennedy and was awarded the UN Peace Medal.

Casals drilled structure and consistency into Greenhouse. During their practice of Bach's *Cello Suite No. 2 in D minor*, he dictated the fingerings and bowings his apprentice was to use. After three weeks of being forced to mimic Casals's technique, Greenhouse began to feel Casals was forming him in his own image. He said pointedly to him, "Mr. Casals, I am concerned I will end up being just a poor imitation of you" (Janof, 2016). Unconcerned by his apprentice's protest, Casals instructed Greenhouse to put his cello down and listen to him; he then went on to change all the bowings and fingerings that he and Greenhouse had worked on over the previous twenty-one days. Greenhouse was speechless. It was then Casals said, "Now that's the real lesson of how to play Bach. You must learn it so well that you remember every single idea you that have had in your practice. Then you forget everything and improvise" (ibid).

Casals had a profound impact on Greenhouse's development as a cellist. Greenhouse recounted how improvising after weeks of consistently practicing exact bowings and fingerings was quite difficult. During his solo career in New York, it took him an entire year to learn the fingerings and bowings to the point where he felt he could improvise as he played. It is this "Casalian" juxtaposition of structure and unconstraint that allowed Greenhouse to infuse his music with his own personal flavor.

MAESTROS TRANSMIT KEY INTANGIBLES TO BUILD A BETTER YOU

Greenhouse had been eager to train under Casals. He knew the great maestros transmit the intangibles that help apprentices to develop a musical style that allows audiences to feel the emotions of the music. He spent two years with Casals before moving back to the US. There he went on to have a successful career and is regarded as one of the greatest American cellists of all time. He was a founding member of the Beaux Arts Trio (cello, violin, and piano), one of the world's foremost chamber ensembles. Greenhouse died in 2011 at the age of ninety-six. He had carried on his maestro's legacy in the form of a fierce commitment to teaching. He worked at the Manhattan School of Music, the Juilliard School, Stony Brook University, and Rutgers University.

Greenhouse's passage through the phases of an apprenticeship:

Phase	Description
Deep observation (passive mode)	Greenhouse observes Casals playing the cello, learning his fingerings and bowings.
Skills acquisition (practice mode)	Greenhouse mimics Casals's fingerings and is able to compare his playing to Casals's.
Experimentation (active mode)	During his later solo career in New York, Greenhouse spends a year learning fingerings and bowings until he reaches the point where he feels he can improvise as he plays.
Mastery	Greenhouse exercises his skills by forming and playing with the Beaux Arts Trio. He also works at the Manhattan School of Music, the Juilliard School, Stony Brook University, and Rutgers University.

TACIT LEARNING

During Greenhouse's two-year apprenticeship, Casals taught him many lessons that helped him hone his craft and impacted his formation as an artist. The most important transfer of knowledge, however, took place tacitly, by osmosis if you will. As Greenhouse sat at the feet of one of the greatest cellists of all time, he was able to observe and discern the true secrets of what made Casals great. For Greenhouse, this revelation was the importance of individuality in music. As he put it,

We must develop a freedom of expression that is personal, that has nothing to do with what we hear others do. There are special techniques for making music that have to be learned, and can be used to create one's own musical style. These techniques are difficult to learn today because those who studied with the really creative and individualistic artists of our past, like Casals, Szigeti, and Enesco, are largely gone, and not around to fight the trend toward musical uniformity. In my own teaching, I am trying to revive an interest in the technique of phrasing and music making so that talented musicians can put their fantastic technique to good use (Janof, 2016).

By watching and observing Casals, Greenhouse picked up what he considered to be the maestro's true genius, what he described as Casals's artistry and personal freedom of expression. By sitting with Casals, he engaged in the transfer of tacit knowledge.

By watching and observing Casals, Greenhouse picked up what he considered to be the maestro's true genius, a personal freedom of expression. By sitting with Casals, he was engaging in the transfer of tacit knowledge.

Tacit knowledge is a term coined by Michael Polanyi, a polymath who did pioneering research in chemistry, economics, and the social sciences. Polanyi asserts, "We can know more than we can tell" (Polanyi, 2013). Tacit knowledge is knowledge, skills, ideas, and experiences that are not easily transmissible; it is implicit knowledge or "know-*how*"—that is to say, practical knowledge of *how* to do something, as compared to explicit knowledge or "know-*what*" (facts).

Harald Bentz Høgseth, who writes extensively on the history of apprenticeships, notes tacit knowledge is personal, and culture and community influence how an apprentice acquires knowledge. He notes, "Not only do apprentices learn the proper movements, tools, treatments, and procedures of the trade, but also the learning process shapes their character, and thus is true enculturation" (Høgseth, 2016).

Enculturation is the process by which people acquire knowledge and values that enable them to become functioning members of their society. It is an important factor in developing mastery in any field. According to E. Adamson Hoebel, enculturation is "both a conscious and an unconscious conditioning process whereby man, as child and adult, achieves competence in his culture, internalizes his culture, and becomes thoroughly enculturated" (Hoebel, 1972).

As in the case of Greenhouse and Casals, Høgseth posits the apprentice must submit to the master, expert, or authority; he notes knowledge is established through the interaction of apprentice and master, student and professor. According to Høgseth, tacit knowledge is the foundation for knowledge through action; it enables us to learn, know, and perceive (Høgseth, 2016: 62).

Soft skills such as leadership, problem-solving, communication, and interpersonal skills are best transmitted tacitly and are most effectively acquired through observational learning.

Hard skills such as technical abilities, on the other hand, can be more easily acquired through individual hard work and study. As mentioned earlier, the key to accelerating the acquisition of complex skills is to assume the mindset of an apprentice and be willing to imitate what you see.

Just like how Greenhouse did not want to become a poor copy of Casals, you may be concerned that imitating a master could prevent you from developing or discovering your own authentic voice. I would argue, however, imitating an expert does not impede creativity; rather, it helps you to innovate and eventually bring something unique to the table. In the next chapter, I will take a more in-depth look at why, for beginners, imitation is better than emulation.

CHAPTER 4

To Ape or Not to Ape? Imitate, Don't Emulate... in the Beginning

---

By three methods we may learn wisdom: first, by reflection, which is noblest; second, by imitation, which is easiest; and third, by experience, which is the bitterest.

CONFUCIUS

In 1887, twenty-year-old Frank Lloyd Wright arrived in Chicago. He was among the throngs of aspiring and ambitious architects who flocked to the city to rebuild the metropolis after the Great Chicago Fire of 1871, which had destroyed over three square miles of the city (Cavalieri, 2010). Wright's timing was fortuitous as Chicago, at that time, was a sort of nineteenth century Silicon Valley of architecture. Young architects were creating innovative and bold designs and building massive commercial structures. Known as the Chicago School, they were constructing fireproof structures using stone, iron, and steel instead of wood. In 1885, with the erection of the Home Insurance Building, they brought to the world the modern skyscraper. At ten stories and one hundred thirty-eight feet, the building was small compared to today's standards, but in the nineteenth century, it was the first skyscraper constructed with steel framing, safe elevators, wind bracing, and plumbing, a building method that would become the standard for skyscrapers across the US and the world (History.com, 2018).

Wright completed two semesters of civil engineering at the University of Wisconsin–Madison and then moved to Chicago and entered this vibrant environment of innovation. After initially securing a job as a draftsman with the architectural firm of Joseph Lyman Silsbee and then working as a designer with Beers, Clay & Dutton, he landed the opportunity of a lifetime with Adler & Sullivan. This firm, founded by Dankmar Adler and Louis Sullivan in 1883, was one of the top architectural firms in the city, and it needed extra hands for its work on Chicago's Auditorium Building. The company was responsible for constructing more than one hundred buildings, many of which became American architectural landmarks.

Wright was offered the job, and instead of working with a junior person, he was given the opportunity to work directly with the firm's named partner, Louis Sullivan. Sullivan, an Irish American who was born in Boston in 1856, was regarded as the "father of skyscrapers" and the "father of modern American architecture." He was described by his employees as highly temperamental and arrogant, a man who lost contracts because he refused to compromise his ideals.

Wright proved he could keep up with this highly talented and prickly genius.

The pair quickly developed a close relationship, one akin to father and son. Louis had no biological children, and Frank's parents had separated when he was fourteen years old, so he lacked a father figure. Sullivan also immediately recognized Wright's ability and took him under his wing. Wright, for his part, ever the eager apprentice, would call Sullivan "Lieber Meister" (Dear Master).

The Lieber Meister took great interest in his apprentice's personal well-being. He ensured his economic stability by giving him a five-year employment contract. In addition, when Wright requested a loan of five thousand dollars (about 153 thousand dollars today), Sullivan granted it without question. He also agreed to hold the mortgage on a house Wright had designed for his growing family. The house was architecturally so impressive it caught the attention of other families, and by 1890, three years after the apprentice had arrived in Chicago, he was sitting in an office next to his master.

The firm of Adler & Sullivan focused on commercial buildings. Busy with many projects, Sullivan and Wright worked extremely long hours. Based on his apprentice's demonstrated ability to get work done, the master soon promoted him to chief draftsman. The firm took on residential projects, such as the homes of clients, only as special requests, and Sullivan gave these projects to Wright, who thus got the opportunity to hone his skill at home design. Historian Robert Twombly has suggested Sullivan used to dictate the form and motifs of these residential projects, and Wright's role was to detail the designs from Sullivan's sketches. Nevertheless, whether these projects were wholly Wright's designs or inspired and directed by Sullivan, Wright would work on these residential designs after hours at his home office and, in the process, developed a singular aesthetic with which he has since been associated (Twombly, 1986).

Working with a master who allowed him to take on significant projects, Wright was greatly influenced by Sullivan's architectural philosophy. It is said Sullivan was the first American architect to think consciously about the relationship between architecture and civilization. He famously said "form follows function," by which he articulated his conviction, in addition to expressing its particular function and structural basis, architecture must evolve from, and express, its environment (Britannica, n.d.). He noted,

> When you look on one of your contemporary "good copies" of historical remains, ask yourself the question: not what style, but in what civilization is this building? And the absurdity, vulgarity, anachronism, and solecism of the modern structure will be revealed to you in a most startling fashion (Coles and Reed, 1961).

In the Sullivan-Wright relationship, we see a near-perfect arrangement between two of the greatest architects in American history: the master is able to produce original work, and the talented apprentice stands ready to learn and dependably follow the master's direction. The apprentice, meanwhile, has access to one of the best minds in the industry and has the freedom and space to practice and hone their own skills.

This perfect union, however, did not last long. Sullivan was arrogant, gruff, and temperamental, but Wright himself was overly confident, independent, and ruthlessly ambitious. Despite his contractual commitment, Wright began to moonlight, designing residential properties in his free time. It is not clear if Wright had by this point realized how much his own style had developed, but to Sullivan's eye, Wright's signature was unmistakable.

In 1893, Sullivan noticed a new home near his own townhouse; he immediately recognized Wright's singular aesthetic in its design. Disappointed by Wright's flagrant breach of contract, he confronted his apprentice, and the two parted ways. It was not until 1914 they finally reunited.

Wright went on to open his own practice in Oak Park. He pioneered a new approach to home architecture called the Prairie Style. This uniquely American architectural style was inspired by, and designed to evoke, the wide, flat landscape of the Midwestern prairie. It was a dramatic departure from old European design and marked the launch of a uniquely American aesthetic associated with the beginning of what has been called the American Century. Wright promoted this idea of organic architecture, meaning the structure should look as if it grew naturally from the environment. This brings us back to form and function: Wright learns from Sullivan's ideas on form and function and takes them a step further by declaring "form and function are one" (PBS, 1998).

Frank Lloyd Wright is one of the most celebrated American architects of all time. Eight of his buildings were inscribed in the list of the UNESCO World Heritage Sites. Architecture enthusiasts praise his iconic designs, including the residence in southwest Pennsylvania called Fallingwater and New York's Guggenheim Museum. UNESCO refers to his buildings as innovative solutions to the needs for housing, work, or leisure and describes them as having had a strong impact on the development of modern architecture in Europe (UNESCO World Heritage Centre).

Historians note Sullivan was very important to Wright's development in that he inspired Wright to push the boundaries of architecture, and he himself modeled this kind of innovation during Wright's apprenticeship.

Frank Lloyd Wright's passage through the phases of an apprenticeship:

Phase	Description
Deep observation (passive mode)	Louis Sullivan dictates the form and motifs of residential projects.
Skills acquisition (practice mode)	Wright details the designs from Sullivan's sketches.
Experimentation (active mode)	Wright designs a home for his family that becomes a showcase which catches the attention of other families. He begins to moonlight, designing residential properties in his free time.
Mastery	Wright opens his own practice in Oak Park and pioneers a new approach to home architecture called the Prairie Style, a uniquely American style inspired by, and designed to evoke, the wide, flat landscape of the Midwestern prairie.

DON'T BE AN APE—IMITATION, EMULATION, AND AUTHENTICITY

Frank Lloyd Wright, when asked about Louis Sullivan's impact on his work, admitted, "Naturally, Sullivan's work influenced me, [his designs] were influencing everybody in the country." When asked whether he felt American architecture had progressed over the past several years, he answered he did not feel it had, adding,

> *I think the effects have been sought and multiplied and the real cause at the center of the thing seems to have languished. If they once mastered the inner principle, infinite variety would be the result. No one would have to copy anybody else. And [to] my great disappointment, instead of emulation, what I see is a wave of imitation (Manufacturing Intellect, 2019).*

As in the case of Louis Sullivan and Frank Lloyd Wright, exceptional apprentices paired with extraordinary masters often go on to produce culture-shifting and boundary-challenging masterpieces. In the exchange of tacit and explicit knowledge, the master invariably imparts a piece of their DNA to the apprentice. As an apprentice increases in skill, they may struggle with the question of imitation and its impact on their own authenticity. We saw this in the previous chapter when cellist Bernard Greenhouse worried about becoming merely a poor copy of Pablo Casals. This concern is legitimate, especially among people who are determined to become masters in their own right by introducing creative innovations and advancements. To achieve this goal, many books and well-meaning individuals encourage young people to pursue authenticity at all costs; they are advised to not "behave like apes." Even the verb "to ape" is derogatory, defined by Google as "to imitate the behavior or manner of (someone or something), especially in an absurd or unthinking way" (Google, n.d.).

But...could we have it slightly backward? Yes, authenticity is important, but hear me out. When you are new to a field, you do not need to be overly concerned about authenticity; rather, you should be obsessed with learning, and learning happens through imitating—not emulating—the master. But, before I get too far ahead of myself, let's look at how cognitive psychologists define imitation and emulation.

Despite the associated stigma, in the purest sense of their meaning, imitation and emulation are forms of social learning. (Recall in Chapter 2 we looked at observational learning in the context of Albert Bandura's social learning theory.)

Harvard scholars Alberto Acerbi, Claudio Tennie, and Charles L. Nunn (2010) define imitation as "copying [the] *action* of a demonstrator (i.e., the behavioral processes leading to the products)," and emulation as "copying [the] *results*, or environmental outcomes, of demonstrations (i.e., the products of behavior)" (emphasis mine).

Michael Tomasello, an American developmental and comparative psychologist and professor at Duke University, has studied imitation and emulation in human children and primates. He notes emulation is a process whereby the observer learns more from the results of the actions than from the details of the behavior of the actions' modeler (Tomasello, 1998).

Andrew Whiten and R. Ham (1992) define imitation as that which occurs when an observer learns the specific aspects of the form from the modeler; the observer then tries to reproduce the modeled behavior as closely as possible.

Imitating thus involves observing, paying close attention to, and copying actions and behaviors, while emulation is only concerned with copying results.

Frank Lloyd Wright's opinion architects were emulators rather than imitators suggests emulation should involve better cognition, more reflection, and a higher level of processing power. Cognitive psychologists, however, tell us the reverse is true.

CHIMPS VS. CHILDREN

In a famous study on imitation and emulation in chimpanzees and children, Victoria Horner and Andrew Whiten looked at the respective tendencies of children and chimpanzees to use either imitation or emulation when observing a person using a tool to remove a prize from a puzzle box (Horner and Whiten, 2004). The experiment involved the demonstrator employing relevant and irrelevant tactics to retrieve the reward, including almost silly actions such as first tapping the box with a stick and poking a false ceiling inside the box. The experiment had two parts. The first part involved an opaque box where the children and chimps were unable to see the inner mechanism of the box; this made it impossible for them to discern which actions were relevant and which ones were irrelevant. The second condition involved a transparent box where it became evident which actions were necessary and which ones were unnecessary to retrieve the prize (twmanne, 2011).

The findings were astonishing. Under the opaque-box conditions, both chimpanzees and children copied all of the steps to open the box; however, under the clear-box conditions, the human toddlers copied the relevant and irrelevant steps faithfully, but the chimpanzees omitted the extraneous steps in securing the reward. Clearly, the children imitated and, to a degree, over-imitated, whereas the chimps emulated. Horner and Whiten (2004: 1), in their summary, stated further,

> These results suggest emulation is the favored strategy of chimpanzees when sufficient causal information is available. However, if such information is not available, chimpanzees are prone to employ a more comprehensive copy of an observed action. In contrast to the chimpanzees, children employed imitation to solve the task in both conditions, at the expense of efficiency.

These results do not mean chimpanzees are more strategic and efficient than human toddlers. On the contrary, the distinction boils down to the difference in cultural learning between chimpanzees and children and suggests the children's over-imitation strategy had great merit in the long run in terms of problem-solving.

Michael Tomasello concluded while chimpanzees do learn things from observing others use tools, they are actually not learning as much as expected. It is precisely because they prefer to emulate, "[to] learn the effects on the environment that can be produced with a particular tool [that] they do not actually learn to copy another chimpanzee's behavioral strategies." He goes on to note, "In contrast, human beings learn from conspecifics by perceiving their goals and then attempting to reproduce the strategies the other person used in attempting to achieve those goals—truly cultural learning, as opposed to merely social learning" (Tomasello, 2000).

Tomasello says further,

> *This small difference in the learning process leads to a huge difference in cultural evolution; specifically, only cultural learning leads to cumulative evolution in which the culture produces artifacts—both material artifacts, such as tools, and symbolic artifacts, such as language and Arabic numerals—that accumulate modifications over historical time. Thus, one person invents something, other persons learn it and then modify and improve it, and then this new, improved version is learned by a new generation— and so on across generations. Imitative learning is a key to this process because it enables individuals to acquire the use of artifacts and other practices of their social groups relatively faithfully, and this relatively exact learning then serves as a kind of*

ratchet—keeping the practice in place in the social group (perhaps for many generations) until some creative innovation comes along. Each human child, in using these artifacts to mediate its interactions with the world, thus grows up in the context of something like the accumulated wisdom of its entire social group, past and present. (…) This kind of learning can be referred to as cultural learning because the child is not just learning things from other persons, but is learning things through them—in the sense that he or she must know something of the adult's perspective on a situation in order to learn the same intentionally communicative act (Tomasello, 2000).

ADVANTAGES OF IMITATION

Imitation thus has its advantages in terms of accelerating learning; there are also benefits to blindly following someone. Children imitate so faithfully because they trust the experience of the adults, a phenomenon Connor Wood considers to be a crucial survival tactic. He notes the best way to master bow-making is by observing successful hunters doing so and assuming every step is critical. When the master hunter waxes his bowstring with two fingers and touches his ear, you copy him exactly, because you don't know if there is a hidden reason for what seem like irrelevant and irrational steps (Wood, 2020).

Skipping steps could be detrimental. Mark Nielsen and Cornelia Blank of the University of Queensland note exact copying is a safety mechanism. Omitting a step in the process of preparing food just because it seems arbitrary, they explain, could have serious consequences: You never know if the purpose of that step was to remove toxins (Nielsen and Blank, 2011).

In "Imitation as a Mechanism in Cognitive Development: A Cross-Cultural Investigation of Four-Year-Old Children's Rule Learning," Zhidan Wang, Rebecca A. Williamson, and Andrew N. Meltzoff (2015) note "a particular benefit of high-fidelity imitation is it increases learning opportunities." Even if acts are not fully understood, children who are able to imitate them in precise detail gain opportunities to discover a deeper meaning and cognitive understanding of the acts, which are first grasped only in a more superficial manner. They argue "action imitation can spark cognitive change" (ibid: 2). The powerful conclusion of their study was action representation and imitation may be key mechanisms for the rapid acquisition and spread of generalizable skills, knowledge, and customs in human cultures.

The research therefore seems to suggest it is advisable to imitate indiscriminately when you are new to a field and that later, with some experience, you can emulate and innovate.

IT'S THE WHO, NOT THE WHAT

One last word on imitation. In "Imitation in Young Children: When Who Gets Copied Is More Important Than What Gets Copied," Nielsen and Blank reported on research that introduced a slight spin to the toy retrieval experiment.

Preschoolers watched two adults retrieve a toy from a box; one adult included irrelevant actions and the other did not. Each of the adults in turn left the room while the children reproduced the action. The researchers found the children reproduced the actions of the adult who stayed in the room; that is to say, when the only-relevant-actions adult stayed in the room, the children performed the efficient retrieval, and when the irrelevant-actions adult stayed, the children performed the irrelevant actions as well (Nielsen and Blank, 2011).

Faithful copying thus not only allows for an accelerated transmission of skills; it also is a manifestation of group alignment. We are, after all, social beings. In the next chapter, we will look at why *who* we choose as masters is more important than *what* we do.

CHAPTER 5

Prioritize the "Who" over the What and Where

Sandy wasn't a mentor in the traditional sense (...), In the sense of people giving you advice and sitting you down. That's what most people mean. I got none of that. Sandy was much more sink or swim and he just shed people left and right who didn't meet his standards, but it wasn't really a mentoring thing. He had a tremendous work ethic, and he was always thinking about how the world was going to change. He was brave and bold. I learned a tremendous amount from him. (...) To do the deals that we did? I look back at those and think, "God, Sandy, you had guts."

JAMIE DIMON

Jamie obviously has far fewer blind spots than most people in this business. He's outperformed most of them.

SANDY WEILL

Even Sandy Weill would admit that he has never been much of a teacher, and that if Dimon wanted to learn the ins and outs of the business, it was largely up to him to be a self-starter. Luckily for Dimon, he was exactly that.

DUFF MCDONALD

In 1974, during his sophomore year at Tufts University, Jamie Dimon wrote a groundbreaking economics paper analyzing the merger of Wall Street securities firm Hayden Stone with brokerage and investment banking firm Shearson Hammill. He argued the merits of combining the efficient Hayden Stone—run by mergers and acquisitions genius Sandy Weill—with the inefficient Shearson. While Dimon had insider knowledge of the transaction, as his father was at the time a broker at Shearson, his analysis nonetheless was quite impressive for a sophomore.

Dimon's mother, Themis, thought her son's paper was brilliant and was eager to share his work with Sandy Weill, who was a close family friend. Weill, having read the young man's paper, told Themis he had not viewed the merger from Jamie's fresh perspective. He sent the undergraduate a personal note congratulating him on a terrific paper and asked permission to share it with others at the firm. Jamie was excited and responded affirmatively, and ever the negotiator, he took the opportunity to request a summer job. Just like that, an economics term paper passed on from a doting mother to an impressed CEO (and family friend) landed Dimon a summer internship in Shearson's consumer business.

Fueled by his insatiable quest to learn, and leveraging the ties between the Dimon and Weill families, Jamie was able to quickly improve his understanding of the business world. Whenever the Weill and Dimon families got together, Jamie would bombard Sandy with questions about the inner workings of his firm. Weill recognized the ambition, fire, and pure intellectual curiosity in Dimon and wanted to harness it. Dimon was attracted to the shrewd, hard worker who was willing to grant him access to deal- and decision-making rooms, where he could see how the masters got things done.

MEET THE MASTER—SANDY WEILL

Sandy Weill was indeed a master who earned his stripes the hard way as a Wall Street outsider. The son of Polish-Jewish immigrants, he was the first of his family to earn a college degree, graduating from Cornell University with a Bachelor of Arts in government in 1955. He got his start on Wall Street at the very bottom of the Bear Stearns' back office, starting out as a runner delivering securities certificates to other firms, making thirty-five dollars a week. He then moved up to quote boy, where he would punch stock symbols whenever a trader would yell for a price quote on a stock. Sandy observed the brokers to whom he provided information and decided to take the brokerage licensing examination. Most people consider the client-facing brokers in the front office to be occupying the sexy and enviable position atop the food chain; Sandy, however, was more interested in the less glamorous hum of the back office where all the operations— accounting, record-keeping, settlements, compliance, and IT—took place. He never lost sight of its importance.

Sandy studied for the brokerage license exam on his own time, passed it, and became an official licensed broker at Bear Stearns. Technically, he could then build his own clientele, buying and selling stocks on their behalf, but instead he spent those early days in his comfort zone, sitting at his desk reading financial statements and Securities and Exchange Commission (SEC) disclosures. At the urging of his wife, Joan, he eventually put down the reports, came out from behind his desk, and "hit the streets." He began to build his client base among the people he had known in his Brooklyn neighborhood. Sandy's superior research skills and ability to identify rare gems earned his clients a lot of money, and his roster thus grew exponentially.

Weill went on to become the cofounder of a small brokerage firm called Carter, Berlind, and Weill, and over a twenty-year period, he made a series of successful and aggressive acquisitions that allowed him to build the securities brokerage firm of Shearson Loeb Rhoades, second in size only to Merrill Lynch. In 1981, he sold Shearson to American Express, where he served as president and chairman of the executive committee.

THE APPRENTICESHIP THAT WOULD CHANGE THE
AMERICAN FINANCIAL SYSTEM

In 1982, when Jamie graduated from Harvard Business School, Sandy invited him to join American Express as his assistant. Jamie turned down lucrative offers from Goldman Sachs, Morgan Stanley, and Lehman Brothers to accept Sandy's invitation, aware he would work for less money but would gain more experience and would enjoy more access to action on the front lines. Thus began the fifteen-year run of one of the greatest examples of apprenticeship in the American financial sector. Dimon and Weill would go on to make history with groundbreaking mergers and acquisitions that reshaped Wall Street and arguably even the American financial system.

Jamie went everywhere with Sandy and was allowed to speak up and present in rooms with men decades his senior. Given Sandy's sink-or-swim philosophy, Dimon was given all the responsibility he was capable of handling. At American Express, he accompanied Sandy and Bill McCormick, another senior American Express executive, to San Francisco with the mission of turning around the American Express subsidiary, Fireman's Fund, which had an excessively large back office. Together they turned the company around by firing 15 percent of the employees and raising premiums. Fresh out of graduate school, Dimon was in the room making decisions and learning on the fly; meanwhile, his counterparts at Morgan Stanley were crunching numbers for the people who would walk into the room to make the deals. Duff McDonald, in his book *Last Man Standing*, noted the immense benefit gained by Dimon from choosing to work with a master instead of with Wall Street's impressively named banks and hard-to-turn-down salaries:

> *Dimon felt he'd made the right decision as well. Most MBAs toil in obscurity for years before they get their shot at the big time. Dimon was immediately exposed to deal-making at its highest levels. (...) Around this time, Dimon reported to Tufts that he was vice president and assistant to the president of American Express. He described his job as "exhilarating, demanding, and a lot of fun." There was no doubt it was demanding, especially considering there'd been no training program or guidebook to help him navigate his entrée into the world of high-stakes deal making (McDonald, 2010: 37–38).*

More important than the exposure to high-stakes deal-making, mergers, and acquisitions, Jamie also had a front row seat with an unobstructed view on the politics of people, ego management, and the way the monied wage war. His apprenticeship with Sandy at American Express afforded him an education in people and psychology that can take most executives decades to learn. He reflected to Weill, regarding his assessment of the politics among American Express's upper echelons, "Corporate America is full of children, and it's a waste of f---ing time" (Langley, 2004: 131).

BETTING THE HOUSE ON THE MASTER

Despite Sandy's success up to that point, American Express actually represented a trough in his career. Biographer

Monica Langley described his role during this period as "President without Portfolio," reflecting the fact the titles of president and chairman of the executive committee were hollow and powerless.

The politics in the executive ranks resulted in Sandy being pushed out of American Express in 1985. Jamie, however, was offered a job with American Express, but he decided to follow Sandy into unemployment in the hope of gaining more experience and being rewarded for his loyalty. McDonald notes during that period, Jamie did question his decision, admitting, "I was looking into the abyss a little bit, pretty much a kid who was not getting experience nor making money in the meantime (…), of course I thought I might have made a mistake" (McDonald, 2010: 46).

Jamie had bet the house on Sandy and on the chance to continue cutting his teeth on real work. He got that opportunity in 1986, when Sandy staged Phase One of his comeback by buying the commercial credit division of Control Data. Again, employing his go-to tools of focusing on the back office and deploying rigorous cost-cutting measures, Weill was back in the game, signaling to the market he had come to win; in 1993, he reacquired his company, Shearson, from American Express. Jamie's gamble to go with Sandy paid off. Dimon was named CFO of Commercial Credit at age thirty, and at age thirty-five, he was named president of Primerica. Jamie was no longer participating in deal-making discussions *with* Sandy; he was now leading those discussions *on behalf of* Sandy. He had demonstrated mastery of Weill's proclivity for scrutinizing the details of a company's finances and expenses, and he had a laser eye for detecting waste.

THE END OF THE APPRENTICESHIP

By 1998, through a series of strategic mergers and acquisitions, Sandy had created the mammoth Citigroup, at the time the largest financial services company in the world. Jamie's genius was undeniable, and as his star rose, he began to emerge from behind Sandy's shadow, becoming a master in his own right. In the process, cracks developed in the relationship. To rein Dimon in, Weill limited the scope of his leadership by creating frustrating co-CEO positions when it was obvious to all Dimon wanted and deserved to run the show completely. Thirty days after the formation of Citigroup, at the pinnacle of the fifteen years of work Weill and Dimon had done together, Sandy fired Jamie.

McDonald sums it up by observing,

> *Weill later concluded perhaps he gave the young man too much responsibility too soon, inflating an ego that would cause Dimon problems in getting along with others. At the time, however, having such an ambitious and intelligent aide more than outweighed the frustration of putting up with his impatience (McDonald, 2010: 35).*

Likewise, Sandy reflected,

> *Still, I felt sick given all that we had accomplished together. Jamie had wanted me to treat him as an equal partner, a desire for recognition [that] I understood but was unwilling to satisfy. I was nearly twenty-five years his senior and (...) his demands for*

equal treatment were disproportionate with what he
deserved (…). I brought Jamie along quickly and in
doing so probably gave him a sense of entitlement
which discouraged him from building a consensual
managerial style (…). My real mistake, though, was
that I had repeatedly missed the chance in our early
years together to curtail his aggressive behavior and
mentor him into becoming a team player (ibid: 175).

McDonald, however, counters,

From Dimon's perspective, it's important to under-
stand that this confidence in his own instincts made
it nearly a given that he wasn't going to be satisfied
with being a great assistant coach. Yes, Sandy Weill
did have the vision. And yes, Jamie Dimon was the
operations guy. After the Citigroup merger, though,
there was nothing left to do but integrate the two
companies. Dimon could be forgiven for coming to
the conclusion that the company was no longer in
need of Weill's particular skills but desperately in
need of his own. And if that had been the case, why
shouldn't the title have come with the job? (ibid: 177)

In March 2000, Jamie became the CEO of Bank One, which
was purchased by JPMorgan in 2004. In 2005, he was named
CEO of JPMorgan. Under Dimon's leadership, which focused
on managing risk and waste management, JPMorgan became
a leading bank in the United States. It was able to distin-
guish itself from all others by mostly avoiding the missteps
of the subprime debacle that caused the Great Recession of
2008/2009.

Financial journalists are obsessed with the Sandy Weill–Jamie Dimon relationship, and many posit Citigroup could have avoided losing two hundred billion dollars in stock market value and cutting one hundred thousand employees in 2008 due to its poor risk management and overexposure to the subprime mortgage crisis if Jamie had succeeded Sandy and not been fired ten years earlier.

Jamie Dimon's passage through the phases of an apprenticeship:

Phase	Description
Deep observation (passive mode)	Jamie has unlimited access to the rooms Sandy went into/commanded and can observe and learn how deals are made.
Skills acquisition (practice mode)	Sandy allows Jamie to speak up and present in rooms with men decades his senior.
Experimentation (active mode)	Dimon is named CFO of Commercial Credit at thirty years old. As a decision-making member of the executive team, he has a central seat at the table and is making deals together *with* Sandy. Then, as president of Primerica, Jamie becomes responsible for making deals *on behalf of* Sandy.
Mastery	Having been fired from Citigroup, Jamie becomes CEO of Bank One in 2000. According to the *Harvard Business Review*, the company had reported a loss of 511 million dollars in that year. Well trained by Weill to obsessively control operational costs, Jamie cancels company-paid country club memberships, car services, supplemental pension plans, matching gift grants, and newspaper and magazine subscriptions. By 2003, the bank reports a profit of 3.5 billion dollars (Locke, 2020).

***

THE *WHO* IS MORE IMPORTANT THAN THE *WHAT*

Every year, thousands of extremely talented young men and women graduate from business schools, but few get the opportunity to access the inner chambers of Wall Street's deal-making rooms. Jamie Dimon was intelligent and had a robust work ethic, an Ivy League degree, privilege, and connections (even a mother who shamelessly planted his term paper with friend and CEO Sandy Weill); all of these played a significant role in securing him early opportunities. Wall Street in the 1980s was also a place where someone like Jamie could expect a golden ticket to the top: He was smart, hard-working, confident, well-connected, male, and white. He was also savvy, discerning, and wise. Plus, he had an apprentice's mindset. At the beginning of his career, he prioritized learning and skill acquisition over the appearance of prestige. This single decision gave him an all-access pass that accelerated his development of critical skills and moved him to the front of the line. When you are working on multi-billion-dollar mergers at age twenty-five and commanding and demanding accountability from people twenty or thirty years your senior and with decades more experience, you effectively have the ingredients for assured meteoric success.

Experience takes time to accumulate. The apprentice mindset, where possible, prioritizes strategic relationships, experiences, and learning opportunities. When you are assessing job options, the apprentice mindset places the "who you will be working with" among your top three considerations. Salary, titles, and prestigious company names are of course important; however, in the long run, they will not accelerate skill acquisition the way working with a master will. An apprenticeship allows access to people and rooms that offer opportunities to observe and pick up on the skills needed to move to the next level.

Dimon understands the value of an apprenticeship to career success. In April 2021, he was among the most vocal CEOs on the need for employees to return to the office after months of remote work due to the coronavirus pandemic. In his 2020 shareholder letter, he noted, "Most professionals learn their job through an apprenticeship model, which is almost impossible to replicate in the Zoom world" (Dimon, 2021). Whether or not you attribute his stance to his age, he is advocating for the proximity of novices to masters in order to accelerate skill acquisition.

A final point on this topic: once you land the job with a master, you should be intentional about learning by observation, that is, paying attention, retaining what you have learned, reproducing actions that yield desired results, and having a motivation to do so. Masters—it is worth noting—are human beings and therefore not perfect; you are thus observing not only for what you *should* imitate but also what you should *not* imitate. When you work closely with someone, you will see their strengths, genius, and prowess; you will also be exposed to their weaknesses and insufficiencies. From Sandy, Jamie learned to keep an eye on the future. He described Sandy as "always thinking about how the world was going to change. He was brave and bold. I learned a tremendous amount from him. (…) To do the deals that we did? I look back at those and think, 'God, Sandy, you had guts'" (McDonald, 2010: 180); however, Dimon also learned how *not* to manage a senior team, remarking he learned to "not hog the spotlight so much your senior team feels underappreciated" (ibid: 179).

CONFIDENCE AND THE CONCEPT OF SELF-EFFICACY

A critical factor I have not yet mentioned is the role of confidence and a sense of self-efficacy in a successful apprenticeship. For this, let us return to Albert Bandura and his social learning theory and observational learning. You will recall the four factors in observational learning are: (1) attention, (2) retention, (3) reproduction, and (4) motivation and reinforcement. We have so far seen how the first three factors work. The fourth factor, motivation and reinforcement, is about the internal and external drivers that underlie the apprentice's willingness to even attempt to imitate or reproduce what the master has created.

The key to the internal driver is what Albert Bandura calls self-efficacy—the belief you will one day attain the same, or higher, level of skill as the master. A high level of self-efficacy is critical in successfully completing an apprenticeship, as it takes an enormous amount of effort, discipline, and hard work to achieve mastery.

According to Bandura, self-efficacy is "people's beliefs in their capabilities to produce given attainments" (Bandura, 2012b). He notes,

> *Unless people believe they can produce desired effects by their actions, they have little incentive to undertake activities or persevere in the face of difficulties.*

> *Whatever other factors serve as guides and motivators, they are rooted in the core belief one has the power to affect changes by one's actions. This core belief operates through its impact on cognitive, motivational, affective, and decisional processes (Bandura, 2012a).*

In other words, our sense of self-efficacy determines what goals we go after. Bandura explains there are four sources of self-efficacy:

- *Performance accomplishments* (or mastery experiences): Bandura notes mastery experiences or personally experiencing success—for example, achieving difficult goals— help to build one's sense of self-efficacy and increase perseverance. In the case of Jamie Dimon, he experienced early success at Tufts when his term paper landed him an internship with Sandy Weill.

- *Vicarious experience* (this comes from models): Watching someone—a master—succeed at something difficult motivates the observer to believe they have the skills needed to achieve the same goal. As Bandura says,

   > *Seeing others perform threatening activities without adverse consequences can generate expectations in observers that they, too, will improve if they intensify and persist in their efforts. They persuade themselves that if others can do it, they should be able to achieve at least some improvement in performance (Bandura, 1978).*

Jamie watched Sandy navigating his unemployment period after he was pushed out of American Express. Later, he was able to draw on those lessons when he had to rebuild and relaunch his own career comeback after Sandy fired him from Citigroup. Bandura cautions watching someone fail at a task can also lead to doubt of one's skills.

- **Verbal persuasion** (verbal encouragement to believe one has the skills necessary to succeed): This can help in overcoming self-doubt. Bandura notes, "People who are socially persuaded they possess the capabilities to master difficult situations and are provided with provisional aids for effective action are likely to mobilize greater effort than those who receive only the performance aids." He cautions, however, "to raise by persuasion expectations of personal competence without arranging conditions to facilitate effective performance will most likely lead to failures that discredit the persuaders and further undermine the recipients' perceived self-efficacy" (Bandura, 1978).

- **Physiological states** (how one perceives and interprets stressful situations): The point here is how we perceive our emotional arousals influences our beliefs and sense of self-efficacy. Bandura notes,

    Stressful and taxing situations generally elicit emotional arousal that, depending on the circumstances, might have informative value concerning personal competency. (...) People rely partly on their state of physiological arousal in judging their anxiety and vulnerability to stress. Because high arousal usually

debilitates performance, individuals are more likely
to expect success when they are not beset by aversive
arousal than if they are tense and viscerally agitated
(Bandura, 1978).

Jamie Dimon's smarts, keen observation skills, and positive sense of self-efficacy allowed him to land on his feet after his apprenticeship ended. It was the soft skills that he developed over the years, however, that really helped him to solidify himself as "one of the world's most influential people," according to *Time Magazine* in 2006, 2008, 2009, and 2011. In an interview with Miles Fisher, Dimon stressed the importance of relationship building and soft skills, noting, "I return every phone call, every e-mail everyday (…), I respond so people know I saw it" (*Blamo Media*, 2020). When asked what class he would teach to college students, he responded categorically: "How to think."

In the next chapter, we will look at the importance of developing soft skills, including relationship management and critical thinking.

CHAPTER 6

Develop Soft Skills: Build the Interpersonal Skills and Personal Traits Needed to Succeed

——

Walk with the wise and become wise.

PROVERBS 13:20 (NIV)

The 1960s New York nightclub and music promotion scene is where we find a rather peculiar apprenticeship pairing of a Russian–Jewish mobster from Chicago and a twenty-something African American with a ninth-grade education from Climax, North Carolina. Master Joseph G. Glaser (known as Joe Glaser), a successful artist manager, would impart to apprentice Clarence Avant the skills that would turn Clarence into a formidable kingmaker, negotiator, and dealmaker.

Joe Glaser was a tough and well-connected agent and businessman who was born in 1896 in Chicago. His father was a Russian–Jewish physician. Intending to follow in his father's footsteps, he entered medical school but dropped out after fainting in an operating room. He then turned to building a business career, starting out as a used car salesman. Glaser became a successful boxing promoter who was notorious for fixing fights. He then became a saloon and club owner and founder and president of the Associated Booking Company, which he cofounded in 1940 with Louis Armstrong. He successfully managed the careers of many top musicians (many of whom were African American), including Louis Armstrong, Billie Holiday, Duke Ellington, B.B. King, and Barbra Streisand.

Glaser was a controversial and complex man. The agent was known for his fatherly approach to his clients, taking care of all aspects of their lives from taxes to dental bills. As Louis Armstrong put it, "Asking me about Joe is like askin' a chile 'bout its daddy. That's what he is. He's my daddy" (Jones, 2016). At the same time, Joe was an alleged notorious mobster who ran Al Capone's Chicago South Side prostitution ring and faced numerous legal challenges related to his treatment of young girls.

Joe understood the levers of power and was a tough negotiator. He would tell new acquaintances, "You don't know me, but you know two things about me: I have a terrible temper, and I always keep my word" (Hodgson, 2016).

He died in 1969 of a stroke, leaving behind a complicated legacy. Contemporary critics who look back on the period do not know whether to characterize him as being ahead of his time regarding race relations—given his work with the greatest Black jazz artists of all time—or to cast him as an exploiter of Black talent. One thing remains certain: Regardless of his motives, Joe held a lot of keys, and he used them to open doors for others, one of whom was Clarence Avant, dealmaker, record producer, and advocate for Black artists.

Prior to the 2019 Netflix documentary *The Black Godfather*, Clarence Avant's name was not broadly known. Avant is considered the celebrity's celebrity; he has come to be known as one of the most influential dealmakers in the business.

Avant was born in 1931 and grew up in the tiny town of Climax, North Carolina. The eldest of eight children, Clarence never met his father and despised his stepfather who abused his mother. He was forced to leave home and move to New York at the age of fifteen after his stepfather found out Clarence had put rat poison in his food.

In New York, Clarence lived with some family members and got a job at Macy's. He did not know what he wanted to be and was open to trying things out. He said, "I didn't know what the hell I wanted to be; I just decided try this, okay, work for a while, try this, and you keep going, you'll hit something" (MOtv Network, 2011). A fellow North Carolinian gave him a job as the weekend manager of Teddy Powell's Lounge, a nightclub in Newark, New Jersey.

One day, Joe Glaser visited the Teddy Powell lounge and observed Clarence arguing with Dinah Washington, a singer Joe represented. Amused and impressed with Clarence's raw and unharnessed negotiating skills, he talked Clarence into getting into show business as a manager. Joe Glaser recognized Avant's ambition and drive and decided to take him under his wing. Under Joe's tutelage, Clarence developed his skills as a manager and negotiator. He would go on to successfully manage and represent singer Little Willie John.

At some point in their relationship, Joe recommended Clarence manage Lalo Schifrin, the Argentinian-American pianist, composer, and arranger who famously wrote the score for *Mission Impossible*. Clarence didn't believe he could or should manage a white man and said to Glaser, incredulously, "What am I gonna do with Lalo Schifrin? He's a white guy." To this Glaser retorted, "What the f* are you talking about— you can sell anything" (Barker, 2016). Joe saw Clarence simply as a negotiator, salesman, and powerbroker; he did not see his race as limiting him. Clarence, likewise, recognized the tremendous learning opportunity he had from being in Glaser's company. He remarked, "I don't ask Mr. Glaser questions. I just learn from him" (Netflix, 2019).

Clarence recalls Joe made him feel comfortable in his Black skin around white people at a time when overt discrimination and racial prejudice were more socially acceptable. He noted,

> *Mr. Glaser would have me go with him to these dog shows, and you've got to imagine I was the only Black person at the g*damn dog show. He also had these sixteen seats behind the visiting dugout at Yankee Stadium, and whenever he'd take me, I would try to walk to the back row, and he'd grab me and say,*

"G*damn it, sit your ass up here with me" (Barker, 2016).

Sitting with Joe at dog shows, Clarence got to observe just how white power brokers made deals. Sitting with them, he heard conversations, watched mannerisms, and learned the game. Cathy Hughes, founder of Radio One and TV One, says, "[Clarence] was like a sponge; he absorbed the best of everybody he saw" (Netflix, 2019).

Moreover, the boldness and fearlessness Glaser cultivated in Clarence *vis-à-vis* white executives would come to serve him as a dealmaker. James Brown said of Avant, "White folks, just generally respect him, they are scared of that n*r" (ibid). It was this boldness that propelled Avant to march into the office of the CEO of Coca-Cola to secure an endorsement deal on behalf of baseball legend Hank Aaron as he was about to break Babe Ruth's record. Avant walked into the office and announced, "[N]*rs drink Coke too" (ibid). He got Hank the deal, netting him far more money than he had ever earned as a professional baseball player.

Emboldened by Glaser's support, Avant would shatter many glass ceilings for Black businesspeople. When he moved to Los Angeles, Glaser helped him and his family to become one of the first Black families to move into Beverly Hills, and he introduced him to the key players in California. Avant went on to purchase the first Black radio station, start two record labels that represented both Black and white artists, and become an influential gatekeeper for Black artists in Hollywood. President Obama said of him, "Clarence exemplifies a certain cool, a certain level of street smarts and savvy that allowed him to move into worlds nobody had prepared him for and say, 'I can figure this out'" (Netflix, 2019).

Clarence attributes his success to Glaser. He credits Joe Glaser with not only opening doors but teaching him everything he knows about the business, noting, "Glaser taught me how to think. He wasn't an educated man, but he was brilliant" (Barker, 2016). It was Avant's ability to think—cultivated by Glaser—that led former-president Bill Clinton to place extremely high value on his advice, saying of him, "His advice per word is worth more than anyone I ever dealt with" (Netflix, 2019).

Journalist Nick Charles of NBC News summarized Avant's rise to success well, writing, "The journey of Avant from a son of the segregated South, who never went beyond the ninth grade, to the corridors of cultural and political power is testament to an indomitable will and the magic of what some dismiss as a soft skill—the building and maintaining of relationships" (Charles, 2020).

Clarence Avant's passage through the phases of an apprenticeship:

Phase	Description
Deep observation (passive mode)	Clarence observes how Joe negotiates by accompanying him to dog shows and baseball games.
Skills acquisition (practice mode)	Avant represents and manages singer Little Willie John. He also manages Lalo Schifrin, the Argentinian-American pianist, composer, and arranger who famously wrote the score for *Mission Impossible.*
Experimentation (active mode)	Avant purchases the first Black radio station and starts two record labels, which represent both Black and white artists.
Mastery	Avant solidifies himself as an influential gate-keeper for Black artists in Hollywood. He also negotiates a lucrative deal with Coca-Cola for baseball legend Hank Aaron when Aaron was about to break Babe Ruth's record.

SOFT SKILLS

Soft skills are the interpersonal and people-oriented skills that allow us to manage people and get things done. The soft skills Nick Charles recognizes are largely due to Glaser's involvement in Avant's life. Avant's daughter, Nicole, former ambassador to the Bahamas, unequivocally credits Joe Glaser's early intervention in her father's life with his success, commenting,

> *All of us need somebody in our lives with an umbrella, with a true word or a kind word or a harsh word to get us back on track. (...) My father had mentors, thank God, in the very beginning like Joe Glaser. If Joe Glaser [hadn't mentored] my father and [taught]*

him the world and take[n] time to open doors for him,
we definitely would not be having this conversation
(Charles, 2020).

As we saw in Chapter 3 with cello apprentice Bernard Green-house and master Pablo Casals, higher-level skills are trans-ferred tacitly from master to apprentice. In the case of Avant and Glaser, Glaser passed on critical people skills Avant would use to propel himself to a successful career. Clarence learned strategy, fearlessness, and grit from Joe.

Business leaders have come to a consensus that, when it comes to recent college graduates, well-developed soft skills are more important to them than the actual degree the new recruit has earned. In a 2015 survey conducted by Hart Research on behalf of the American Association of Colleges and Universities (AAC&U), it was noted cross-cutting soft skills such as written and oral communication, teamwork, ethical decision-making, critical thinking, and the ability to apply knowledge in real-world settings are more important to an individual's success at their company than his or her undergraduate major (Hart Research Associates, 2015).

The World Economic Forum report entitled "The Future of Jobs Report 2020" considered the outlook of jobs and skills in the next five years. Among its key findings, it concluded skills gaps continue to be high, noting employers have identified skills gaps in critical thinking and analysis, problem-solving, active learning, resilience, stress tolerance, and flexibility (World Economic Forum, 2020).

World Economic Forum's
Top Five Skills for 2025:

1. Analytical thinking
2. Active learning and learning strategies
3. Complex problem-solving
4. Critical thinking and analysis
5. Creativity, originality, and initiative

Similarly, the *Financial Times*, in its FT 2018 Skills Gap survey, identified the top five most difficult skills to recruit as: (1) ability to influence others; (2) strategic thinking; (3) drive and resilience; (4) big data analysis; and (5) the ability to solve complex problems (Nilsson, 2018).

The skills gap is a matter of global importance. One key takeaway from the March 2020 US Chamber of Commerce "Hiring in the Modern Talent Marketplace" study was 74 percent of American business leaders agree there is a lack of skilled talent within the available workforce (US Chamber of Commerce Foundation, 2020). Given the seriousness of the skills gap and its implications for the global economy and for individuals' abilities to find employment, many have placed the blame on universities for churning out young adults who are ill-prepared and lack the basic requisite skills. Cheryl Oldham, vice president of education policy for the US Chamber of Commerce and senior vice president of education and workforce at the US Chamber of Commerce Foundation, noted, "As a nation, we need to move toward a skills-based approach for educating and hiring where the skills taught in the classroom directly align to the skills required for a career" (US Chamber of Commerce).

This posture and thinking have led educators, business leaders, and students to evaluate the role higher education should play in preparing students for the job market. QS Quacquarelli Symonds, an organization that provides analytics and insights to the global higher-education sector, asked the critical question, "Should universities make employability their central focus or do employers need to accept a degree of responsibility for shaping new hires to meet their needs?" They concluded while some skills will be learned or fine-tuned in the workplace, universities play a role in equipping students not only with the technical skills required for the chosen career, but the sought-after soft skills as well (James, 2021).

High-value competencies and soft skills that businesses require are, I believe, best developed on the job and not via one-off classroom trainings with PowerPoints or three-day conferences in Vegas using contrived scenarios. These critical skills are primarily transmitted the way human beings have always transmitted life and death competencies—person to person through deliberate and sustained contact between a master and an apprentice.

The key to distinguishing oneself as a new hire is demonstrating the ability to learn the skills and competencies that make one irreplaceable in the workplace and in demand in the job market. The good news is these competencies and soft skills are not industry- or even job-specific; they can be learned and developed even without knowing what you want to do with your life. Critical thinking and analysis, problem-solving, active learning, resilience, stress tolerance, and flexibility are all soft skills that can be developed in any sector.

As you learn and develop soft skills and start to deploy them, only the feedback you receive will let you know how well you are doing. Feedback will not always be positive—it will sometimes be harsh and difficult to accept; nevertheless, the apprentice mindset requires you are able to handle criticism and can govern yourself accordingly. In the next chapter, we will examine how apprentices manage and grow through tough criticism.

CHAPTER 7

Welcome and Seek Out Tough Feedback

———

It takes humility to seek feedback. It takes wisdom to under-stand it, analyze it, and appropriately act on it.

STEPHEN COVEY

In the field of higher education, Dr. Gail Whitaker is known among her peers and by direct reports as a compassionate, driven, and people-oriented leader. A curious lifelong learner, she is quite lettered, with two doctorates, three master's degrees, and a bachelor's degree. She has held numerous senior-level positions in academia, serving as the dean of the business schools of both Colorado Technical University and Virginia International University. Earlier in her career, she was chief technology officer at the National Council of La Raza. As of writing of this book, she is the founder and director of The Learning Continuum, a curriculum development and professional training company that designs and builds curricula for universities, NGOs, and private sector companies. Despite her professional and leadership achievements, she describes herself as an educator whose life's mission is empowering people in their God-given purpose.

A native Washingtonian, Gail has had the good fortune of working with many masters who instilled in her the importance of leadership and team development. She says her most influential apprenticeship took place when she worked as an IT executive at the National Board for Professional Teaching Standards (NBPTS), reporting to Dr. Gary Galluzzo, the former executive vice president.

As of writing this book, Dr. Gary is professor emeritus at the College of Education and Human Development and the director of the PhD in Education program at George Mason University. He served as the dean of George Mason's Graduate School of Education and also held board positions with the NBPTS and the American Association of Colleges for Teacher Education. Over the course of his career, he has focused his research on how students become teachers, on curriculum reform in teacher education, and on preparing teachers to be change agents.

A master teacher and leader, Dr. Gary taught Gail some of the most significant lessons she has learned on leadership and people management. She credits him with transforming her from a manager who was focused on tasks to a leader focused on people. She describes him as being patient and a great coach.

THE UNOFFICIAL PERFORMANCE APPRAISAL

During one of Gail's annual performance reviews, Dr. Gary took a very unconventional approach in the way he provided feedback on her work product, skills, and competencies. He first carried out the official performance review process as dictated by the human resources department. As part of that process, Gail provided a written update on the status of her key performance indicators (KPIs), laying out her plans and objectives for the upcoming year. Dr. Gary then reviewed her submission and gave the written assessment that would go in Dr. Gail's HR file. According to this official review, she had met all her KPIs on time and within budget and had delivered outstanding work, and he assured her he was looking forward to working with her in the coming year. At the performance review discussion, Dr. Gary congratulated his apprentice on a successful year. Gail thanked him for his assessment, told him she looked forward to achieving even more in the next fiscal year, and stood up to leave his office. As she did so, Dr. Gary said quietly, "Well, there is one more thing...could we talk for a few more minutes?" Sensing a change in the atmosphere, Gail sat back down, puzzled.

"That was the official performance review for your HR file," Dr. Gary said. Sliding another piece of paper across the desk to her, he continued, "Here is the unofficial performance review that is for your continued development and growth."

Reading the paper, Gail could not believe her eyes: It was a complete 180 degrees from the glowing official assessment— it did not at all glow. It critiqued her leadership pointedly, outlining areas that needed further development. It said she needed to improve her time management skills and empower others more. It observed while she was great at getting her work done, she was working far too many hours at the risk of her health and needed to delegate more tasks to her team. Stunned, she muttered "thank you" and hurried out of the room, totally deflated.

On her drive home, hurt morphed into defensiveness. By itemizing her vulnerabilities and inadequacies so explicitly, Dr. Gary had injured her ego. An overachiever, she had always prided herself on her work ethic, her knack for getting tough things done, and her ability to play well with others. She was not accustomed to failure. Arriving home, she went straight to her office, tossed the letter in a drawer, opened her laptop, and composed her counterargument. She then printed it, put it in an envelope, and scrawled his name on it. The release felt good. She went to bed feeling like she had restored the equilibrium in her world.

Early the next morning, she walked confidently to Dr. Gary's office and knocked casually on the open door. He greeted her with a smile and asked how he could help her. Without speaking, she handed him her response. Dr. Gary calmly took the envelope from her and placed it in the top drawer of his desk. Gail then turned on her heel and, with her head held high, went back to her office. She had redeemed her reputation, re-established her sense of self, and restored her dignity.

Gail felt she had defended the honor of her badly bruised ego, but she still did not feel vindicated. She had a gut feeling that perhaps her boss's observations had some merit. After a week had passed, late one night, she sat down at her desk at home, opened her drawer, and reread Dr. Gary's document. She decided to devise a plan of action, with KPIs to address each growth opportunity he had identified. She developed a growth and improvement curriculum for herself that included reading assignments, signing up and paying from her own pocket for leadership conferences and seminars, and joining associations where she could meet and network with other leaders in the technology field. Her plan was SMART—it was specific, measurable, achievable, realistic, and time-bound. As part of her roadmap, she took a closer look at Dr. Gary's own leadership style. She observed how the master managed all his stakeholders—including his superiors, his colleagues, and his direct reports—and how he managed himself.

As she executed her plan, she began to be better and stronger at work, and it was noticeable to everyone, including Dr. Gary. A year later, he asked Paula, one of Gail's direct reports, to come into his office. He retrieved the still-sealed envelope from his desk and gave it to her with a message: "Give this to Gail and tell her I never read it."

One of Gail's action items was applying to be a mentor with the Women in Technology association. In going through the process of becoming a mentor, one thing led to another, and she was invited to apply to become the chief technology officer (CTO) of the National Council of La Raza, the largest nonprofit advocacy organization for Latinx people in the United States. This opportunity came out of left field while she was working toward being promoted to CTO at her current job at NBPTS. She applied and got the job with La

Raza. When she spoke with Dr. Gary about the opportunity, he told her she should follow her heart.

From Dr. Gary, Gail learned the greatest lesson on leadership and character in her life. He had perfected the delicate balance between handing out tough feedback and extending grace. It was not until she got to the National Council of La Raza she realized Dr. Gary had turned her into a strong leader. In her senior executive position, she encountered numerous challenges that gave her the opportunity to apply the leadership lessons she had learned from him. She was often told she was a natural leader, but deep down she knew, even if that were the case, it had been Dr. Gary who had brought it out in her. Deciding to follow that leadership path all the way to its end and continue to build on the foundation Dr. Gary had laid, she enrolled in a doctoral program in management at the University of Maryland Global Campus.

RECEIVING TOUGH FEEDBACK

Receiving tough feedback can be difficult and humbling. It can leave you feeling vulnerable and deeply deflated. One can emerge from corrective feedback sessions with a bruised ego, feeling angry, shaken, and uncertain about oneself. The technique of sandwiching negative feedback between two pieces of good feedback helps to cushion the blow, but it still hurts. Feeling offended and defensive when people call us to account and force us to confront uncomfortable truths about our inadequacies and failures is natural. Where emotions and egos are involved, it is often hard to separate the message from the messenger, especially when the feedback does not come sugarcoated.

Dr. Tasha Eurich, an organizational psychologist, executive coach, speaker, and *New York Times* best-selling author of the book *Insight*, says feedback is not only a gift, but it is the key driver of performance and leadership effectiveness. She notes negative feedback is particularly useful, as it provides us with important information on the changes we need to make (Eurich, 2018b). In *Insight*, she recommends using the 3R model (receive, reflect on, and respond to) to help process negative feedback as objectively as possible while setting aside our ego and our preconceived notions about ourselves (Eurich, 2018a: 165).

Eurich explains receiving feedback is not merely passively listening; rather, it is an active pursuit where we should seek to understand by asking questions and taking notes. She says this approach gives us valuable information and prevents us from reacting negatively or going into a state of denial. She recommends asking those offering feedback to give examples of the behavior being described. Likewise, reflecting on feedback means chewing on the information before acting on it. Eurich explains, in her experience, people who receive startling feedback often take days or weeks before being able to begin to address the situation. That time period allows one to recognize feedback, while valuable, is also the subjective viewpoint of the person providing it. If you are in a field where ambition and winning are important, behaviors that may be viewed as negative in one context could be beneficial in the larger scheme of things; the problem may be only a matter of degree or intensity, or of knowing better how to harness the behavior.

In your response to feedback, you can decide if you need to change your behavior—as Gail did—or if you need to change the narrative. If you have behaviors that are hampering your progress, you need to change; however, if you are exhibiting characteristics that are essentially positive but are being manifested excessively, or if you are not managing your brand well, you may indeed need to change the narrative. In some instances, certain negative behaviors may be indications of a strength that is being incorrectly expressed; in such cases, the negative feedback may not be indicative of the need to change your behavior, it could simply be a call for better self-awareness, expression, and regulation.

A word of caution: I would be remiss if I did not acknowledge that not all negative feedback is constructive or comes from a genuine place with the goal of building one up. If you suspect someone's feedback is more along the lines of verbal abuse and bullying, then you should seek counsel from others who are familiar with you and your work. The goal of feedback is to help you improve and grow. If this is not what is happening, you should remove yourself from the situation. Hillary Clinton, in her book *Hard Choices*, offers wise words when she says, "I'm often asked how I take the criticism directed my way. I have three answers: First, if you choose to be in public life, remember Eleanor Roosevelt's advice and grow skin as thick as a rhinoceros. Second, learn to take criticism seriously but not personally. Your critics can actually teach you lessons your friends can't or won't. I try to sort out the motivation for criticism, whether partisan, ideological, commercial, or sexist, analyze it to see what I might learn from it, and discard the rest (Clinton, 2014: 168).

GIVING FEEDBACK IS HARD TOO

Dr. Gary, with his feedback, gave Gail an exceptional gift, and she made good use of it. Not many leaders take the time, as Dr. Gary did, to provide that level of detailed information, and getting corrective feedback—even if it hurts—is far better than getting no feedback at all. Feedback is valuable intelligence about how you are being perceived and how you are performing. If you are on a sports team or in a dance troupe and the coach or dance instructor ignores you and never corrects you, this should be a red flag signaling they may not see you as having great potential. Athletes and dancers know receiving and integrating feedback is the only way to get better over a sustained period of time. They are constantly asking how they can improve their shot, make their leaps higher, or create more speed in their turns.

While it stings to receive negative feedback, the person giving it is not having much fun either. According to David Rock, CEO of the NeuroLeadership Institute, as well as Beth Jones and Chris Weller, people experience as much anxiety giving feedback as they do receiving it. This helps explain why so few people give true constructive feedback and why it is such a gift. Rock, Jones, and Weller (2018) note their research shows 87 percent of employees indicate they want to "be developed" in their jobs, but only one-third report having received the feedback they need to improve. They explain many managers dread those conversations because they are unclear on the needs and wants of the employees, and employees, in turn, feel like criticism is an affront to their egos (ibid). In addition, in cultures where age and hierarchy are important, it may be difficult for younger employees to give feedback to subordinates who are older than they are.

SEEKING OUT FEEDBACK

Feedback is normally assumed to occur through the formal channels of the workplace; these are mainly quantitative in the form of KPIs, and qualitative in the form of performance review conversations. While both of these are valuable, it is worth noting feedback is being made available all the time. It is important to be observant and to pick up what is being said around the coffee machine, in casual comments in unguarded moments and in the form of body language. Watch for both what is said and what is left unsaid. In other words, read the air.

In the next chapter, we will explore this notion of reading the air and learning the unspoken and unwritten rules.

CHAPTER 8

Read the Air: Learn the Unspoken and Unwritten Rules

———

You start a church, and you call yourself an apostle. We were outraged. You're a bishop in a year. We were outraged. You broke all the unspoken rules because our generation has unspoken rules; they're not written down anywhere, but if you break one of them, we are kind of salty.

BISHOP T.D. JAKES

In 1997, Sunny Hostin, a Puerto Rican African American lawyer, went for an interview with Judge John R. Fisher for a job in the appellate division of the office of the United States Attorney in Washington, DC. Judge Fisher was chief of the appellate division; he worked extensively on criminal cases in the DC circuit. Landing a job with him was quite impressive for the twenty-nine-year-old Notre Dame Law School graduate. In chapter five of her memoir, *I Am These*

Truths (cowritten with Charisse Jones), Sunny recounts how she had purchased a black and white pantsuit at Ann Taylor that would make her look stylish and professional for her meeting with Judge Fisher (Hostin and Jones, 2020).

As Sunny was sitting in the waiting area for her interview, Brenda Baldwin White, an African American woman who worked at Judge Fisher's office, noticed her and her pantsuit. White approached her, introduced herself, and invited the candidate into her office. She inspected Sunny from head to toe and then looked her square in the eyes and said,

> *You're about to meet with John Fisher (…), that means the job in Appellate is almost yours, but you won't have a shot if you walk into Fisher's office, wearing pants (…). He's very old school, the most old-fashioned guy in this building (…), he won't hire a woman in a pantsuit, you're going to have to change. (Hostin and Jones, 2020).*

Brenda estimated she and Sunny were the same size and offered to let Sunny wear the skirt she was wearing. Aghast at what seemed to her like audacity, Sunny retorted she was not going to put on a skirt just to appease a chauvinist. Brenda calmly picked up the phone and marshalled her other Black female skirt-wearing colleagues to her office. They all advised Sunny not to allow a pair of pants to stop her from getting the job of a lifetime. Sunny acquiesced and changed into Brenda's skirt. She landed the job (Hostin and Jones, 2020).

In 1997, the culture of the Washington, DC, legal society still possessed a certain old-fashioned decorum, with an unwritten rule female lawyers should not wear pants. This was not Judge Fisher's rule, it was an unwritten rule of the "society."

Sunny gained an enormous amount from working with Judge Fisher, who is now a judge on the DC Court of Appeals. As of this writing, she is cohost of the talk show *The View*, as well as senior legal correspondent for ABC News and a best-selling author.

Requiring women lawyers to conform to what seemed like an outdated dress code—even making hiring decisions on that basis—appears to be unfair and, indeed, chauvinistic. It may not be correct, however, to assume it was Judge Fisher himself who was imposing or reinforcing the rule, or that he judged women negatively if they did not conform to it. What appeared to be his bias could have been, instead, his reluctance to hire someone who seemed to be ignorant of the unwritten rule of wearing skirts. If they were that oblivious, he may have thought, how could they be politically adept enough to figure out other more complicated rules?

LEARNING THE UNWRITTEN AND UNSPOKEN RULES

All groups and societies have norms and guidelines for the behavior of their members that dictate what is acceptable and unacceptable; the combination of these norms constitutes the culture of the group. Any "culture"—including the culture of a particular profession or workplace—has its own beliefs, customs, codes (including dress codes), and rules and norms for social interaction.

As they say in the business world, "It's the way things are done around here." Some of a culture's—or subculture's—beliefs, customs, and guidelines are written down in the form of laws, others are maintained through spoken maxims, and still others are in the form of unwritten and unspoken rules. Through the process of enculturation and socialization, these explicit and implicit norms are passed down informally and formally from senior members of a group such as parents, teachers, religious leaders, or managers, to junior members, including children, new converts, and new employees.

The formal laws and rules are easy to learn since they are encoded in written constitutions, handbooks, and well-known sayings. The unwritten and unspoken rules, which usually involve social behavior, can be equally important within the group; however, they are trickier. Everyone who has been in the group for some time has been in one way or another "initiated"—they know the rules. No one speaks of them, though. They are just in the air.

DINING TABLE SOCIALIZATION

Unwritten and unspoken rules are often learned in safe and intimate spaces, what I like to call "learning around the table." It is during family mealtimes children learn table manners and social graces and get clarity around societal norms that may not make sense to them. Parents often teach these rules through corrective measures. Children learn not to chew with their mouths open, how to use silverware, and what appropriate dinner conversation topics are. They listen to conversations and overhear comments from adults that elucidate hidden societal rules. They absorb these norms and apply them at home and in the broader community.

When you enter a new group, you must understand no matter how insignificant they may seem, the obvious and hidden cultural norms are what govern the group. The key to mastery is showing the awareness to, first, acknowledge there are rules to learn, and then pay close attention to the members of the group in order to pick up on those rules. Failure to do so signals to the group you are not one of them or you do not deserve to be one of them; this could lead to missed opportunities. On paying attention to the unspoken rules in a new job, Robert Greene advises apprentices,

> You will be observing two essential realities in this new world. First, you will observe the rules and procedures that govern success in this environment—in other words, "this is how we do things here." Some of these rules will be communicated to you directly—generally the ones that are superficial and largely a matter of common sense. You must pay attention to these and observe them, but what is of more interest are the rules that are unstated and are part of the underlying work culture. (…) The second reality you will observe is the power relationships that exist within the group: who has real control; through whom do all communications flow; who is on the rise and who is on the decline (Greene, 2012).

A point to note is some unspoken or unwritten rules are not benign. They support some of the most insidious and exclusionary forms of oppression in society, such as the seven isms:

racism, sexism, classism, elitism, ableism, ageism, and heterosexism. Thus, I am in no way suggesting here unspoken and unwritten rules should always be accepted and embraced for a coveted entry pass to a club. Systems and codes that promote and support injustice and inhumane policies and practices should by all means be rejected and dismantled; however, you cannot accept, embrace, or even challenge and change something until you understand it.

READING THE AIR

In Japan, there is a concept known as *kuuki o yomu*, or reading the air. Japanese culture is what Erin Meyer, INSEAD business school professor and author of *The Culture Map*, classifies as a "high context culture." In high context cultures, communication is nuanced and messages are implied and not plainly stated. In low context cultures such as the United States and Germany, by contrast, communication is explicit and clear, and messages are meant to be taken at face value (Meyer, 2016). Clearly, in Japanese culture, the ability to read the air is critical to success.

In Japan, someone who is unable to read the air is referred to derogatorily as being "KY" (*kuuki ga yomenai*); they can be socially shunned as a consequence. In 2019, the tweet of a Japanese businessman from Tokyo with the Twitter handle "@da_masu" went viral. In a 2020 BBC report on this phenomenon, @da_masu recounted a rather embarrassing story of being KY during a meeting with a potential client in Kyoto, which is considered the cultural capital of Japan. During the meeting, the client had complimented the businessman's watch; flattered, @da_masu had prattled on about the watch's features. Only later did he realize the client had actually been communicating the meeting had gone on long enough and it was time for him to wrap up his little spiel.

In this BBC report, Shinobu Kitayama, editor for the *Journal of Personality and Social Psychology* and professor at the University of Michigan, commented on @da_masu's faux pas and on the complexity of reading the air, saying, "Often times, [in Japan] you'll be kicked out from important discussions in many organizations. [...] If you find [reading the air] stressful, that's a problem" (Lufkin, 2020).

While the Japanese example is somewhat extreme, what we can take away from the story is when we are on the verge of, or in the process of, violating an unwritten or unspoken rule, people around us give us cues in the form of glances, body language, or coded messages; these messages are obvious to those who know the rules.

How, then, do we avoid finding ourselves in embarrassing or career-threatening situations? How do we avoid breaking rules of whose existence we are not even aware? The not-so-simple answer is some of these rules will—unfortunately—be learned by trial and error. You will want to do as much of your learning as possible in a safe, low-stakes space. Your observational skills and relationships will stand you in good stead as you learn to read the air:

- Do as much of your learning as possible in a safe, low-stakes space.

- Observe interactions and relationships sharply, watching for power dynamics and body language.

- Pay attention, imitate, and ask questions.

- When you walk into a room with people you do not know, identify who is not new to the situation and follow their lead.

UNIVERSAL UNWRITTEN AND UNSPOKEN RULES IN A BUSINESS ENVIRONMENT

While all groups have their idiosyncrasies, there are indeed some rules that apply universally to the business world.

Gorick Ng is a Harvard University career advisor who specializes in coaching first-generation, low-income college students; he is also a former Boston Consulting Group (BCG) management consultant and author of the best-seller *The Unspoken Rules: Secrets to Starting Your Career Off Right*. In the book, Ng defines the unspoken rules of work as being the particular ways managers expect things to be done which they do not explain; top performers, Ng says, intuitively do things right. I highly recommend this book to all entry-level employees. Three of his key points are quite applicable to an apprentice mindset; they include,

- *"Show you want to learn and help."* Ng notes when you are new to a team or project, people expect you to ask questions and be in "learner mode" (Ng, 2021: 2). Over time, he says, they will expect you to know what's going on and to make thoughtful contributions; this is what he calls "leader mode" (ibid). This is, effectively, the ability to demonstrate one has an apprentice mindset and the capacity to observe, imitate, reproduce, and then achieve mastery.

- *"Mirror Others."* Ng recommends when you are in unfamiliar settings you should find people you respect and relate to and then observe how they dress and write; then adopt elements of their behavior and performance that seem authentic to you and which you admire. He further explains you should also mirror the urgency and seriousness of the people with whom you are working. When interacting with someone who has leverage over you, Ng says, you should show more urgency and seriousness. When in doubt, he advises, let others go first (Ng, 2021: 5). Stay calm, I would add. Chaotic and frantic energy makes you appear frazzled and panicked; it can be distracting and disruptive and can suggest to people you are not good at working under pressure. Employ the duck technique: Appear to glide calmly on the surface even while your feet are paddling furiously beneath the water.

- *"Recognize patterns."* Ng advises new employees should avoid making the same mistake twice. You should look for patterns among your superiors that allow you to anticipate their requests or instructions: If they always ask for X, have it ready before they ask (Ng, 2021: 5). This advice echoes the phases of an apprenticeship: deeply observe the behaviors and patterns in your environment; acquire the skills that will enable you to know, and even anticipate, what your superiors want; and experiment with providing the item or work before they ask for it, or performing the task in advance.

Once you are able to look and sound like the masters and can begin to internalize and imitate their habits, you signal to the market you are part of the club, a master. In the next chapter, we will look at how delivering like a master will show you are now a full member of the mastery society; we will see how that open doors.

PART III

CHAPTER 9

Learn Fast, Work Hard, and Deliver Results

———

I may not always be the smartest person in the room, but no one will outwork me.

ROSA WHITAKER

The May 13, 2000, cover issue of *The Economist* magazine called Africa the hopeless continent. It harshly remarked, "The new millennium has brought more disaster than hope to Africa. Worse, the few candles of hope are flickering weakly" (*The Economist*, 2000). While the British periodical offered this grim outlook for the continent, on the other side of the Atlantic, the United States was announcing to the world that it indeed saw hope and a future for Africa. On May 18, 2000, President Bill Clinton signed the African Growth and Opportunity Act (AGOA) into law. AGOA is the cornerstone of the United States' trade policy with Africa. With a stroke of his pen, President Clinton changed US foreign policy with Africa from one based primarily on aid to one that included trade and investment; with that, he signaled to the global market that Africa should not be ignored.

Flanking President Clinton for this historical sea change in US–Africa relations were AGOA's parents, the master, Congressman Charlie Rangel, and his apprentice, Rosa Whitaker. They beamed with pride to see the culmination of more than four years of negotiations with Democrats, Republicans, unions, the American private sector, and African heads of state result in a comprehensive trade policy that, in the years since, has created millions of direct and indirect jobs in sub-Saharan Africa and more than one hundred thousand jobs in the United States (Agoa.info, n.d.).

AGOA began when Rosa, as an economic officer at the American Embassy of Côte d'Ivoire, was tasked with convincing African finance ministers to join the World Trade Organization (WTO). In speaking with West African top-ranking officials, she realized there was no incentive for them to join. At the time, Africa was considered to be an economic and trade wasteland that was of interest primarily for the extraction of its subsoil resources and as a recipient of charity and foreign aid. Frustrated with what was felt to be an antiquated and ineffective policy approach toward Africa, Rosa Whitaker, Mike Williams (who was chief of staff to then Congressman Jim McDermott), and like-minded colleagues came up with the idea of drafting policy on trade between the United States and the countries of sub-Saharan Africa. Rosa then decided to return to Washington, DC, from Côte d'Ivoire with the goal of changing the US policy stance toward Africa. She knew of only one person who had the political will and muscle to make it happen—Congressman Charles (Charlie)

Rangel. She understood any African American who wanted to move things in and from Washington, DC, needed to do so with the power cover of a true and respected master and consensus builder. Charlie Rangel was just that.

THE MASTER

Congressman Rangel was a smooth and charismatic New Yorker who served in the House of Representatives from 1971 to 2017. During that time, he distinguished himself as one of the most influential African Americans in Congress. He was a founding member of the powerful Congressional Black Caucus; he was also the first African American to chair the important House Ways and Means Committee, which has jurisdiction over the government's budget, that is to say, taxes, tariffs, social security, Medicare, and other revenue-raising measures. An outspoken bridge builder, Rangel is known for his pragmatism and smooth negotiating skills, with a reputation for getting tough things done by finding compromises to win over his colleagues and opponents. For half a century, Congressman Rangel won all his re-election bids with over 90 percent of the vote. He was beloved by his constituents and by those around the world for his push for justice. He was vocal about the drug issue plaguing the streets of New York, supported Soviet Jews, advocated for the Low-Income Housing Tax Credit, and successfully pushed for anti-apartheid sanctions, achieving what became known as the Rangel Amendment. Congressman Rangel also has a Purple Heart and a Bronze Star for his service during the Korean War and remains a well-respected political leader who is admired for his ability to make friends out of enemies and build consensus.

Many of Rangel's apprentices have gone on to have successful careers in politics and business. Rosa stands out among them for the significant amount of political capital he expended on her.

THE APPRENTICE

Rosa was born and raised in Washington, DC, in the shadow of the Capitol Building. She developed an apprentice mindset at a young age. She understood early on the power of the legislature, as attending Congressional hearings had been her hobby and passion from the time she was fourteen years old. She volunteered with Democratic politician and activist Nadine Winter, where she learned the art of persuasive writing. She received her bachelor's and master's degrees from American University's (AU) School of Public Affairs.

While at AU, Rosa became very interested in Africa. In 1980, Canaan Banana, the university's former chaplain, became the first president of Zimbabwe (formerly Rhodesia). Banana gave a speech at AU and invited students to volunteer and help to build the new country. After graduation, Rosa moved to Zimbabwe and lived with a local family. It was there she began her apprenticeship on Africa, learning about the continent around the dining table. It was there she learned how to read the African air, discovering the social rules and relationships that drive how business and political deals were won and done on the continent. Upon her return to the United States, she did a stint as executive director of the Washington DC Office of International Business; this made her the youngest leader of an international business agency for a major US municipality. After this, she joined the US Foreign Service as an economic officer, based in Côte d'Ivoire. Between 1995 and 1997, Rosa served as Congressman Rangel's diplomat-in-residence and senior trade advisor.

THE APPRENTICESHIP

Congressman Rangel was a phenomenal master and Rosa was an eager apprentice. He tasked Rosa with helping to develop the African Trade and Investment Caucus in Congress. She also advised him on the World Trade Organization in its infancy, as well as on relations with Africa and China.

Rosa said later the two years she spent working with Congressman Rangel were among the most important of her career in terms of professional growth. She describes Congressman Rangel as a workaholic who spent his days in meetings and congressional hearings. In the evenings, he would return to his office to review briefing memos and strategize. It was during these evenings Rosa and other staffers would glean insights not only on the follow-up required from the day's events, but also on how Congressman Rangel thought and how he got things done. Under the master's tutelage, Rosa learned the ways in which relationship-building, negotiation, and compromise could flip any adversary. She noted,

In the office of the inimitable Congressman Charlie Rangel, whose footprints have provided major

*inspiration to many people, including me, I learned
a lot. I feel extraordinarily blessed and privileged to
have had him as my boss. The lessons I learned from
Congressman Rangel would fill a book. He is that
rare combination of a dreamer and a doer, and he
taught me while having a dream is wonderful, making it happen is what counts. At his knee, as it were,
I learned the fine art of Washington arm-twisting, of
when to compromise and when not to compromise, of
when to get down into the mud of the trenches and
when to take the high ground. In short, I learned
about politics. A lifelong Democrat, I learned to not
just get along with Republicans but to find common ground with them to achieve a greater good
(Rosa Whitaker).*

Rosa worked hard. She managed multiple and diverse stakeholders on Capitol Hill and in Africa. She learned a lot and
fast. She studied the issues on Rangel's agenda and antici-
pated the kind of briefing memos he needed and the people
he would need to hear from. She quickly developed a reputation for being a consensus-building convener. Her passion
for, and dedication to, Africa was also palpable, which did
not escape Congressman Rangel. He observed how she built
strong relationships on the Hill on both sides of the aisle and
among the African private and public sectors; he noted the
skill with which she consulted with the leading experts on
African trade across the globe. He saw his apprentice had the
capacity, skills, and guts to move things, both within the US
and internationally.

During one of Congressman Rangel's speeches on Capitol Hill, he made a small mistake, causing Rosa to motion not-so-inconspicuously in order to give him the correct information. Rangel, in turn, not-so-jokingly replied, "Rosa, if I'm going to be your puppet, at least hide the strings." Rosa became so good at managing Rangel's fellow congress members she was able to get their views ahead of meetings with him; knowing Rangel's stance on the topics, she even managed to resolve issues prior to his arrival. During one meeting, he reminded her half in jest that even though the members treated her as an equal, she was not an elected member.

Rosa regarded the congressman's remarks as signals she was perhaps overstepping, and she adjusted her approach and pulled back; however, what the congressman and his fellow masters were actually indicating—perhaps unknowingly— was she was no longer an apprentice and was now advancing on the master's journey.

OPEN GATES

One day, Congressman Rangel called Rosa in for a quick chat. He confided in his apprentice he had put her name forward to President Clinton to be the first-ever US Assistant Trade Representative for Africa in the Executive Office of the President. Rosa was worried since she and her colleagues had actually conceived of this position and placed it in the pending AGOA legislation that had been collectively drafted by them, she would be accused of being an excessive self-promoter. According to Rosa later, Rangel "shut down her negative chatter" and paid no attention to her stated concerns about going after the role. Rangel told President Clinton without a doubt there was only one name that should be on the list, and it was Rosa Whitaker's. He had seen firsthand her track record for delivery and her ability to manage stakeholders to get tough things done. Rangel told Rosa he had put her name forward and he was confident she would finish the work they started together on AGOA from within the executive branch of government.

In 1997, Rosa moved to the Executive Office of the President of the United States, taking up a position in the Office of the US Trade Representative (USTR) as the first-ever Assistant US Trade Representative for Africa. At USTR, she got AGOA across the finish line, along with other multilateral trade policy initiatives for Africa during the Clinton and Bush administrations. As she says,

> *With Congressman Rangel, I was extremely fortunate to help craft and work for the enactment of the landmark African Growth and Opportunity Act—or AGOA as it is known. (…) On a deeper level, AGOA represents a whole new paradigm shift in America's relationship to Africa—a paradigm shift away from the old-style financial hand-outs, which have bred little more than dependence on Western largesse, toward a respect for the ability of Africans to determine their own future and solve their own problems. AGOA provides an opportunity, not a guarantee, and while African countries have varied in their ability to take advantage of it, it has undoubtedly advanced the cause of prosperity and economic stability in Africa (Rosa Whitaker).*

Congressman Charlie Rangel was more than a master, mentor, and sponsor to Rosa; he used his keys and political capital to unlock doors for her, including that of the Executive Office of the President. This then led to a whole host of other opportunities. In 2003, three years after AGOA had passed, Rosa left government and opened her own company, The Whitaker Group (TWG). TWG is a corporate strategy, transaction advisory, and project development firm that specializes in Africa. To date, the company has facilitated more than one billion dollars in trade and capital flows to Africa, and Rosa is considered one of the world's foremost experts on African trade, investment, and business. For her work in Africa, *Foreign Policy Magazine* named her one of the Top 100 Global Thinkers in 2010.

NO SUBSTITUTE FOR HARD WORK, RELENTLESSNESS, AND RESILIENCE

The chapters up to this point have focused on how to learn from the master: tacit learning, developing soft skills, receiving tough feedback, and learning the unspoken and unwritten rules.

Yes, an apprenticeship is about learning, but it is also about delivering. Remember, an apprenticeship is a formal, transactional relationship whereby the apprentice learns from the master, but during which it is also required they add value. Masters will expect the apprentice to apply the lessons they are learning to the work they are doing. This is what Rosa did. During her two years with Congressman Rangel, she observed, applied what she learned, and delivered with excellence. Rosa also understood loyalty, something which was highly valued by her master mentor. Rosa rarely shares her success story without mentioning Congressman Rangel, sometimes at length. She still calls him for counsel and notes how much inspiration she draws from what he shares from his deep wells of wisdom, despite being over ninety-two years of age.

Rosa is a frequent speaker at colleges and universities and almost invariably shares with her audience what she calls the five C's of success. These she adopted from her business mentor, Mike Ullman, former chair of Starbucks, during the time she served as deputy vice chair on the board of the global charity Mercy Ships. Rosa's five C's are:

1. *Character*: Have integrity; be credible by being clean and honest.

2. *Commitment*: Be punctual. Show you can be counted on to execute your work with excellence.

3. *Courage*: Achieving great things will come with difficulty and fear. Face fear with tenacity and perseverance. Build up the mental toughness to face uncertainty and failure. Do not allow disappointment to stop you.

4. *Competence*: Do what you do well. Competence and charisma are not synonymous: if your perceived competence is greater than your actual competence, you will be pegged as all talk and no action; however, if your actual competence is higher than your perceived competence, you will be underestimated and may lose out on

opportunities. The goal is for your actual and perceived competence to be equal, so work on how you appear professionally.

5. *Confidence*: Believe your goal is within your reach, you have what it takes to achieve mastery, and you can accomplish what you set out to do.

GATEKEEPERS

Solid relationships are the foundation of deal-making in business, diplomacy, and politics. Who you know matters, and who speaks on your behalf—your corridor reputation—matters even more. Rosa often reminds young apprentices that most consequential decisions about your career will be made when you are not in the room. Her most meteoric rise, the move to the Executive Office of the President, was initiated by Congressman Rangel in her absence. Advancement is subjective and is determined by power brokers. In a meritocracy, demonstrated abilities result in being moved into positions of success, power, and influence.

Masters are the ones who assess and defend demonstrated abilities and merit; they are the gatekeepers of advancement, and it is they who determine who gets ahead and who does not. Just as apprentices observe masters with the goal of learning new skills, masters also observe apprentices. They are always weighing and assessing the person under their tutelage and determining whether they are acquiring the skills needed to succeed in the field. The master observes the apprentice's grasp of hard skills, soft skills, and the unspoken and unwritten rules; they also examine their habits and personal traits. Very quickly, a master can determine what the apprentice is capable of, what they are likely to achieve, and if they are displaying the potential for greatness.

That is the goal of apprenticeship: to develop mastery, and eventually to be recognized as a master, take a seat at the table, and use one's acquired skills to leave a mark on the world.

CHAPTER 10

Let's Get Practical—
Starting, Managing,
and Ending an
Apprenticeship

———

You will know when your apprenticeship is over by the feeling you have nothing left to learn in this environment. It is time to declare your independence or move to another place to continue your apprenticeship and expand your skill base. Later in life, when you are confronted with a career change or the need to learn new skills, having gone through this process before, it will become second nature. You have learned how to learn.

ROBERT GREENE (2013)

Isobel Acquah began her professional career in 2003 as a solicitor with the London law firm of Cameron McKenna. She worked for a powerful and demanding South African–English man named Simon Morris who was a master of his craft but quite temperamental. He took Isobel under his wing and committed to her training. He gave her access to rooms, events, and people far beyond her experience and skill. He brought her to high-end client dinners and on corporate trips so she could learn to manage clients. He saw potential in her and pushed her hard. He often called her work rubbish and made her redraft it until it was perfect.

One day, Simon walked into her office and told her she had developed into a fine solicitor, but she lacked hard-core business experience. He gave her the opportunity of a lifetime, one reserved for seasoned attorneys: He sent her on a secondment to a firm that needed a lawyer to assist with some transactional work.

During the secondment period, Isobel started a second apprenticeship with Katherine Ashdown, the lead lawyer for the account. Isobel learned a lot from Katherine and discovered she enjoyed executing large-scale business transactions. She said later Katherine taught her how to think like a client, that from her she had learned to avoid bogging the customer down in lawyerly jargon and instead distilling exactly what they needed. At the end of her secondment period, Katherine asked her to stay with the firm. While Isobel was flattered, her sense of loyalty to Simon compelled her to decline Katherine's generous offer and return to Cameron McKenna. Katherine was disappointed, but she was impressed with Isobel's loyalty. Isobel returned to Cameron McKenna and continued to grow under Simon's leadership and kept Katherine as a friend and mentor.

One evening during a Cameron McKenna weekend retreat, Isobel had an odd encounter with a mysterious blonde lady from the firm's Amsterdam office. The two women had connected immediately and spent hours together chatting and sipping wine. The conversation was progressing well and naturally, when suddenly the stranger blurted out Isobel did not fit in at the firm and should consider a career move. Isobel was not offended; rather, she appreciated the other woman's candor and her sharp observation. This exchange prompted Isobel to start considering her next steps; it was the 2008 recession, however, which made the decision for her, when the company made her redundant and gave her a generous payout. While her colleagues were devastated at receiving their pink slips, Isobel was ecstatic. She called her parents and happily announced to them she had been given a hefty advance that was going to buy her time to figure out the next phase of her life.

A few weeks later, Katherine called to invite her to work with her at Bank of America. Isobel submitted her CV, was interviewed, and got the job. She excelled in her new position. The bank identified her as having high potential and saw her as a rising star, promoting her several times. Life was great. She was living the executive dream. She had a strong network, traveled extensively, lived in a fancy flat in a posh London borough, and was on track to becoming one of the youngest Black, female managing directors in the bank's history.

One day, as Isobel was reviewing a contract, she dropped her pen, and as she bent to pick it up, she heard a voice in her head say, "You're done here." She listened to that voice and decided to walk away from Bank of America, from her beloved boss, and from her career. She did not have a plan; she just knew her apprenticeship was over and she needed to move on.

She took some time off to travel around Asia and Latin America and then moved to Accra, Ghana. There she worked as a transaction consultant, passed the Ghana law bar, and started a mentoring group for young professional women.

As of this writing, Isobel is an associate partner at Globetrotters Legal Africa; a strategic and transactional consultant for various global investors; and an activist for women's rights as the founder and director of the Pearl Safe Haven, an emergency shelter for survivors of sexual and domestic violence. And, by the way, when she got married five years after arriving in Ghana, Katherine flew in from London to be in her wedding party as a Mentor Mama.

LET'S GET PRACTICAL

Isobel landed two apprenticeships, managed both Simon and Katherine well, and ended her apprenticeships without drama. She successfully turned her apprenticeships into mentorships and treasured friendships.

Up until now, the focus of this book has been on establishing the elements of an apprentice mindset: what it is, why it is important, what traits should be nurtured in oneself in order to do it well and gain the most from it, and what proven advantages are seen to have been gained by singular people who enjoyed the benefits of master–apprentice relationships early in their careers. The logical next questions are, okay, what now? And, following from that, how do you land an apprenticeship with a real master? How do you, as an apprentice, manage the master? And, finally, how do you end an apprenticeship? This chapter offers the practical advice and applications that will answer those questions.

STARTING AN APPRENTICESHIP

There are three obvious ways to effectively start or land a valuable apprenticeship:

1. Apply and be accepted

2. Be recruited to a job or volunteer position and accept the mission

3. Be connected to a master who needs assistance in a job or volunteer opportunity

In the first chapter, we established an apprenticeship is a formal relationship whereby a novice gains skills by working with a master. In the twenty-first century, this is most likely to take the form of actual employment, protégé programs, or a formalized volunteer arrangement; in all cases, the time requirement is significant.

In order to assess whether an opportunity will result in a true apprenticeship—and is not just some gig to pay the bills and pass the time—I recommend weighing prospects using the 5Ws+1H method: Who, What, When, Where, Why, and How. Before that, however, let me underscore for you to be accepted, invited, or recommended to work alongside a master, you must first be able to show potential in an area in which the master needs help. You should walk in the door with a sufficient level of hard skills and the basic soft skills that will allow you to hit the ground running. Again, an apprenticeship is a transactional relationship; believing you are there to just learn and not produce will end your apprenticeship very quickly, as you will be dead weight and a waste of time.

- **WHO: Are you prioritizing the who over the where?**
  When you are trying to build skills and learn, who you work with or for is more important than where you work. With this in mind, choose someone who is a "master." They should be an expert in their field or an expert at the skill(s) you are looking to acquire, but they will not necessarily be the most senior person on the team. When you are starting out, you may of course not have access to such people, but you do want to work with someone who is excellent at what they do. Before you go into the interview, google the company and the team. Do your homework. Familiarize yourself in advance with the members of the team with whom you would be working; find them on LinkedIn and see what kind of intelligence you can gather before you go in. Once you start work, it will probably take you less than three months to figure out who the stars are; your challenge then is to find a way to work with them. Here's a secret: The most talented people in a company often are working the hardest. Few people turn down free labor, so find a way to lighten their load and you will soon have yourself an apprenticeship. One

caveat: Make sure you are adding value! If they have to slow down to help you, it won't work.

- **WHAT: Will apprenticing with this particular master allow you to gain the skills you wish to learn?** If you do not have a clear view of what you want to learn, focus on the soft skills of critical thinking, problem-solving, writing, presenting, and relationship-building. These can be learned in any domain and are universally valuable; learning them well from a master will allow you to apply them in a versatile way in any situation (recall the chapters "Soft Skills," "Receiving Tough Feedback," and "Learning the Unspoken and Unwritten Rules").

- **WHERE: Will this apprenticeship allow you to "get in the room"?** Once allowed in, you can take advantage of situated learning and of the phenomenon of legitimate peripheral participation (LPP) whereby skills are learned within an appropriate real-life context. LPP allows a progression from observing and performing small but important tasks to greater participation and experience, and eventual membership in the "community of practice"; learning, in short, is a contextual social phenomenon that is achieved through participation (Lave and Wenger, 1991). Jean Lave and Etienne Wenger define situated learning as learning that takes place in the same context in which it is applied. In the corporate context, the office is the community of practice and is where newcomers assimilate norms, behaviors, values, relationships, and beliefs. Masters conduct workshops and create environments where the work—and thus the learning—occurs. Working with an accomplished master in a dynamic environment is a crucible for accelerated learning and skills acquisition. With Simon, Isobel was able to engage in, and benefit from, this kind of situated learning.

- **WHEN should I start? ASAP.** It is never too early or too late to start an apprenticeship. While they are most beneficial at the beginning of your career or during a career transition, as a novice or new hire, you will always benefit from applying the key elements of an apprentice mindset. You will want to start sooner rather than later because of the "ten-thousand-hour rule" that was popularized by Malcolm Gladwell in his book, *Outliers*. Gladwell noted it takes approximately ten thousand hours to master complex skills and achieve mastery. If you engage in deliberate practice for four hours a day, it will take over ten years to achieve mastery.

- **WHY should I undertake a formal apprenticeship?** An apprenticeship will allow you to learn, gain skills, and develop mastery in the context of a formalized relationship, one that makes overt, legitimizes, and structures the status of learner and the role of teacher within the workplace. The master–apprentice relationship makes a space for learning within the work environment; in this relationship, you as the junior person must work hard and show ability but are allowed to not know things. It emphasizes the commitment of both the apprentice and the master to the process of knowledge transfer.

- **HOW do I apply the apprentice mindset?**

  – Engage in observational learning

- Embrace tacit knowledge

- Imitate don't emulate, in the beginning

- Build good self-efficacy

- Develop soft skills

- Receive and seek out tough feedback with an open mind

- Learn the unspoken and unwritten rules

- Put in the work and sweat required to gain skills and mastery

MANAGING THE MASTER

Once you have landed an apprenticeship, you will need to manage the master well. Working with a master will not be easy. True masters are the best of the best: They are experts, innovators, creators, and culture shifters. They believe in excellence, dogged hard work, tenacity, relentlessness, and determination. They have high expectations of themselves and others, so they despise mediocrity, laziness, and excuses. Be prepared to learn, sweat, and grow; be ready to work long hours, take on stretch assignments that are beyond your level of knowledge or skill, and to be told—sometimes not so gently—your work does not meet their standards. But expect also to eventually experience the euphoria of seeing something to which you contributed come to life.

MASTERS AS INSTRUCTORS AND MODELERS

So far, we have focused on what the apprentice must do to make the most of working with a master. We talked extensively about observational learning, acquiring tacit knowledge, and imitation. However, this is not the only way you will learn. There will be times when you will receive master classes in how to get certain things done; the master will seize a teachable moment and show you how to do something step by step. This is what I call the master-as-instructor interactions. Other times the master will consciously model behavior for you to imitate—what I call master-as-modeler. Let us see how this is done by Bishop T.D. Jakes, American author, presidential advisor, filmmaker, and pastor of the thirty-thousand-member megachurch The Potter's House in Dallas, Texas. Jakes is also known for his practical-application–based style of preaching, which emphasizes leadership and providing opportunities for the next generation.

MASTERS AS INSTRUCTORS

Bishop Jakes recounts a story of a time when he was going to give a lesson on preaching to his daughter, Cora, who is an associate pastor at The Potter's House Church. As he tells it,

> *I told her to go out and buy a puzzle (...). I said why do you think they put the picture on the puzzle? She said, so I will know where the pieces go. I said exactly (...), how you place the pieces ultimately should reflect the picture on the box. (...) When you get ready to preach, the Bible is full of pieces; how you construct it should be so artful so when you are*

*finished it looks exactly like what God put in your
mind. And that is what success is. Success is not millions of dollars, it's not millions of people, it's not a
crowd of people. Success is when whatever God put
in your head as a vision appears in front of your face.
That is success and you don't stop until you get it, and
you fight for it, and you stand up for it and you cry
for it, and you labor for it, and you don't give up on
it because God has given you a picture and whenever
God gives you a picture, don't you stop until you get
there. (…) My idea of success is whatever I saw in
my head, I want to see in front of my face" (Jakes,
2022: 01:16:00).*

In 2005, the *New York Times* described Bishop Jakes as one of
the United States' most influential and mesmerizing preach-
ers (Bumiller, 2005). In instructing Cora to purchase a puzzle,
he shared with her the secret to how he has been able—Sunday after Sunday for over forty-five years—to deliver powerful, inspirational, yet practical sermons. At the same time, he
helped her with her sense of self-efficacy by giving her great
advice on how to define success.

MASTERS AS MODELERS

Apprentices are called to imitate while masters are called to
model. Let us look at how Jakes models.

On January 21, 2022, a panel discussion took place which
included Jakes and three men whom he calls his sons. During
that discussion, his son and apprentice Mike Phillips told a
story about his struggles as a first-time author. He told of

how Bishop Jakes had arranged a meeting with his publishers "to set them straight" and that, when Phillips had expressed gratitude to Jakes for standing up for him, Jakes had seized a teachable moment which highlighted the importance of modeling: He told his son he had intended to model how to handle the business world. As Jakes put it during the panel discussion,

> Mentoring is important (...), but modeling is also important. (...) I got all those people on the phone, and I talked to them not just to straighten them out, [but] I wanted you to see how to do it. This is how you do it, this how you face it. This is the language in the literary world. This is how it works. This is what happens in retail. This is what happens in publishing. And when I model it in front of you, then your spirit says, "Oh, I can do it" (Jakes, 2022).

Jakes was signaling the next time something like this happened, Phillips would not need his intervention; he would be able to imitate what he had seen Jakes do and handle the situation himself.

ENDING AN APPRENTICESHIP

Isobel said later without Simon and Katherine, she would have never developed the capacity and confidence to achieve what she had accomplished. At the same time, she believed following that still-small voice to quit when she did gave her the timing that allowed opportunity and chance to collide.

Apprenticeships are not open-ended, and they must inevitably come to an end. The key questions are: How do you know when it is time to end? Who initiates the end? And how do you end it?

The end of an apprenticeship can be precipitated in four ways. It can be:

- **Master driven:** The master decides the apprentice has gained sufficient mastery and it is time to move on.

- **Apprentice driven:** The apprentice feels they have gained sufficient mastery and it is time to end the apprenticeship or move on to another master.

- **A masterpiece has been completed:** The apprentice completes a masterpiece of a quality that signals to the apprentice, the master, and the community of practice mastery has been gained.

- **External circumstances**: External circumstances precipitate the end of the apprenticeship.

In the case of Isobel, we see in one instance her apprenticeship ended when the market/external voices told her it was over. In another case, however, she herself recognized it was time to move on. Getting this right is tricky, as it is different for everyone and there are no if–then formulas or guidelines. Analyzing the apprenticeship stories from previous chapters, however, we can say that:

Apprenticeship Endings

Chapter	Apprentice	Domain	How it ended
1	Leonardo da Vinci	Art apprenticeship with Andrea del Verrocchio	Completion of masterpiece
2	Maureen Magarity	Basketball apprenticeship with Dave Magarity	Market/apprentice driven: Magarity was offered the head coach position of the Women's Basketball team at the University of New Hampshire
3	Bernard Greenhouse	Music apprenticeship with Pablo Casals	Master driven and apprentice driven, when the agreed-upon time period ended
4	Frank Lloyd Wright	Architecture apprenticeship with Louis Sullivan	Master driven, when Sullivan fired him
5	Jamie Dimon	Wall Street apprenticeship with Sandy Weill	Master driven, when Sandy fired him
7	Dr. Gail Whitaker	IT apprenticeship with Dr. Gary Galluzzo	Apprentice driven, when implementing Dr. Gary's feedback resulted in a new job at the National Council of La Raza
9	Rosa Whitaker	Capitol Hill apprenticeship with Congressman Charlie Rangel	Master driven, when Congressman Rangel recommended her for a job in the Clinton administration

Regardless of who initiates the end of an apprenticeship, it is important for apprentices to manage the transition astutely. The end of an apprenticeship signals you are joining the guild of professionals, and you will need to conduct yourself accordingly. Common sense rules include:

- Acknowledge the learning opportunity and show gratitude.

- Remain on good terms and, ideally, in touch with your former master, when possible. Never believe they taught you everything they know or you picked up everything they had to teach. Remember, a lot of what you learned was tacit.

- If you had a bad master, do not burn bridges and do not bad-mouth them. Recognize you can learn just as much from bad behavior as you can from good behavior.

- When you are yourself a master and have your own workshop/business, recruit and accept apprentices with potential so you can train the next generation of leaders.

The end of an apprenticeship is a graduation of sorts. Depending on where you are in your career, the end of one apprenticeship could mean the beginning of another or could mark the transition from student to teacher. When the time is right, accept responsibility for instructing the next generation of learners, modeling the behaviors they should be understanding and adopting, and ensuring you create the right culture for them to acquire mastery.

Conclusion

While it is wise to learn from experience, it is wiser to learn from the experiences of others.

RICK WARREN, *THE PURPOSE DRIVEN LIFE: WHAT ON EARTH AM I HERE FOR?*

For me, writing this book has been a journey of remembering, reflecting, researching, and, ultimately, sharing. My goal has been to demonstrate what became my firm conviction over the years: Adopting an apprentice mindset and entering into an apprentice–master relationship can lead to accelerated skill acquisition on the route to achieving mastery.

- *Observe*: During this phase, observe, observe, observe. Watch closely what the masters do, how they do it, when they do it, and where they do it. Figure out (or ask) why they do what they do. Pay attention to every detail and remember what you have learned.

- *Practice*: Now it is your turn to reproduce what you have observed. Imitate, don't just emulate. Early in your career, you may not have a full understanding of why things are done, so imitate the process; later, when you have internalized the processes, you can perhaps skip stages and emulate end results. Observe and practice actions and processes and you will gain tacit, unspoken knowledge. Practice your skills first in a safe environment; set aside your ego and actively seek out input and feedback from masters. Try your skills—for example presenting and leading groups—in low-stakes environments. Gradually speak up more and take on more central roles in meetings with your colleagues. Learn by simply doing—gradually and when the time is right. Pay attention to when the time feels right.

- **Do:** You are nearing, or have come to, the end of your apprenticeship. You should now have gained versatility in the application of your skills and should be comfortable in a variety of scenarios and domains. You should be executing, in real time, the skills and tasks you have learned. You should be taking on roles, and speaking up, in higher-stakes environments.

You have learned as much as you can learn from your apprenticeship. You are ready to take on bigger challenges, aim for mastery, and, eventually, become master to a new, young apprentice.

Acknowledgments

Thank you to the many people who made this book possible.

To my parents, Betty and Earle: You are my first masters. Thank you for your countless prayers and for always reminding me of whose I am. I love you.

To Kataran and Katarlah: Screw the bulb!

To Aunty Edna: Thank you for your prayers and encouragement.

To my beta readers: Thank you for reading the first draft and providing detailed feedback. I appreciate your perspective and comments. *Isobel Acquah; Sheona Kellman; Patricia Garcia; Susanne Quadros; Dr. Gail Whitaker; and Rosa Whitaker.*

To the book's pre-sale campaign supporters: Thank you for your early support; I'm grateful. *Kok Leong Ang; Carrol Bennett; Helen Blyth; Dana Burgess; Dr. Elvis Burrows; Chi Chi'naya; Magistrate Gwendolyn Claude; Lisa Evanson; Lourdes and Steven Fraser; Patricia C. Garcia; Deborah*

Greenwood; Ariun Khaltarkhuu; Beth King; Hilary Kozikow-ski; Cass Lauer; Ida Miller; Cameron Palmer; Maria Cristina Paraiso; Bobby Patsios; Susanne Quadros; Nicole Rodney; Xaivier Ringer; Sandrine Rukundo; Jessica Smith; Ambassador Yolande Smith; Kaleda Stokes; Harold Taylor; Kataran Taylor; Katarlah Taylor; Dr. Gail Whitaker; Rosa Whitaker; and Harrison and Eileen Wilder.

To the Creators Institute and NDP Team: Thank you, Eric Koester, for creating a visionary platform and for believing in my book's idea during its infancy stage. Thank you to NDP editors Cass Lauer, Kathy Wood, and Linda Berardelli for keeping me on task and schedule.

Appendix

───

INTRODUCTION

Derler, Andrea, Anthony Abbatiello, and Stacia Sherman
    Garr. "Better Pond, Bigger Fish." *Deloitte Review* 20 (2017).
    https://www2.deloitte.com/content/dam/insights/us/arti-
    cles/3611_Better-pond-bigger-fish/DR20_Better%20pond%20
    bigger%20fish_reprint.pdf.

CHAPTER 1

Apprenticeship.gov. *Jumpstart Your Career Through Apprentice-
    ship.* United States Government: Apprenticeship.gov. n.d.
    https://www.apprenticeship.gov/career-seekers.

Apprenticeship.Gov. *Industry-Recognized Apprenticeship
    Program.* n.d. Accessed February 26, 2022. https://www.
    apprenticeship.gov/employers/industry-recognized-appren-
    ticeship-program

Bundesagentur für Arbeit. "Apprenticeships in Germany."
    Video, 5:37. June 23, 2016. https://www.youtube.com/

watch?v=7gtYl77l4UQ. ———. "Schritt Für Schritt Zum Wunschberuf - Bundesagentur Für Arbeit." Bundesagentur für Arbeit, n.d. https://www.arbeitsagentur.de/bildung/aus-bildung.

Britannica. Apprenticeship. n.d. Accessed February 26, 2022. https://www.britannica.com/topic/apprenticeship.

Global Times. "China Implements New Apprenticeship Program to Reinforce Talent Training." *Global Times.* June 23, 2021. https://www.globaltimes.cn/page/202106/1226839.shtml#:~:text=In%20principle%2C%20apprentices%20could%20receive.

Greene, Robert. *Mastery.* New York: Penguin Books, 2012. ———. "The 3 Vital Steps of the Apprenticeship Phase." *Huff-Post.* November 8, 2013. https://www.huffpost.com/entry/the-3-vital-steps-of-the-_b_4227085#:~:text=The%20Appren-ticeship%20Phase%2D%2DThe%20Three%20Steps%20or%20Modes&text=These%20steps%20are%3A%20Deep%20Obser-vation.

Hansman, Catherine. "Critical Perspectives on Mentoring: Trends and Issues. Information Series." Washington, DC: Office of Educational Research and Improvement, 2002. https://www.govinfo.gov/content/pkg/ERIC-ED465045/pdf/ERIC-ED465045.pdf.

Harris, Carla A. *Expect to Win: Proven Strategies for Success from a Wall Street Vet.* New York: Hudson Street Press, 2009.

HM Government. *Connecting People With Ambition to Businesses With Vision.* HM Government, UK: Apprenticeships. https://www.apprenticeships.gov.uk/. n.d.

International Labour Organization. "Study on Quality Apprenticeships in Five Countries of West Africa: Benin, Côte d'Ivoire, Mali, Niger and Togo." Geneva: International Labour Organization, 2020. https://www.ilo.org/wcmsp5/groups/public/---ed_emp/documents/publication/wcms_755947.pdf.

Morgan Stanley. Profile: Carla Harris: Senior Client Advisor. Morgan Stanley, n.d. Accessed February 14, 2022. https://www.morganstanley.com/profiles/carla-harris-vice-chairman-of-wealth-management.

Solly, Meilan. "The Man Who Mentored Da Vinci Receives First U.S. Retrospective." *Smithsonian Magazine.* September 13, 2019. https://www.smithsonianmag.com/smart-news/man-who-mentored-da-vinci-has-finally-received-his-first-us-retrospective-180973127/.

The National Gallery of Art. "Andrea Del Verrocchio: A Closer Glook." https://www.nga.gov/features/verrocchio-closer-look.html#:~:text=As%20a%20Florentine%20humanist%20wrote .

The National Gallery. "Andrea Del Verrocchio." The National Gallery, n.d. https://www.nationalgallery.org.uk/artists/andrea-del-verrocchio.

Uffizi Galleries. "The Baptism of Christ." Uffizi Galleries, n.d. https://www.uffizi.it/en/artworks/verrocchio-leonardo-baptism-of-christ.

UNESCO World Heritage Centre. n.d. "The 20th-Century Architecture of Frank Lloyd Wright." UNESCO World Heritage Centre. https://whc.unesco.org/en/list/1496/.

U.S. Department of Labor. "History and Fitzgerald Act" U.S. Department of Labor." n.d. https://Www.dol.gov/Agencies/Eta/Apprenticeship/Policy/National-Apprenticeship-Act. https://www.dol.gov/agencies/eta/apprenticeship/policy/national-apprenticeship-act.

Walther, Richard, and Ewa Filipiak. *Towards a Renewal of Apprenticeships in West Africa: Enhancing the Professional Integration of Young People*. Paris: Agence Française De Développement, Département de la Recherche, 2008.

Word Sense Dictionary. "Apprehendere—WordSense Dictionary." Word Sense Dictionary, n.d. Accessed February 14, 2022. https://www.wordsense.eu/apprehendere/.

Zhang, Kate-Yue, and Jean-Luc Cerdin. "The Chinese Apprenticeship Model: The Spirit of Craftsmanship." In *The Success of Apprenticeships: Views of Stakeholders on Training and Learning*, edited by Jean-Luc Cerdin and Jean-Marie Peretti, 187–92. London and Hoboken, New Jersey: ISTE Ltd and John Wiley & Sons, Inc., 2020.

CHAPTER 2

America East Conference. "#3Pillars || Maureen Magarity's Coaching Story." *Youtube.* December 31, 2015. Video, 1:19. https://www.youtube.com/watch?v=lyXj-7z8fdc.

Bandura, Albert. *Social Learning Theory.* New Jersey, USA: Prentice-Hall, 1977.

Epstein, David. *Range: Why Generalists Triumph in a Specialized World.* London: Macmillan, 2019.

Fox News. "Father-Daughter Coaching Matchup Believed to Be a D-I First." *Fox News.* January 7, 2021. https://www.foxnews.com/sports/father-daughter-coaching-matchup-believed-to-be-a-d-i-first.

Greene, Robert. *Mastery.* New York: Penguin Books, 2012.

Lave, Jean. *Apprenticeship in Critical Ethnographic Practice.* Chicago: University of Chicago Press, 2011.

Toland, Jennifer. "Daughter Knows Best as Holy Cross Women's Basketball Tops Army Again." *Telegram & Gazette.* January 10, 2021. https://www.telegram.com/story/sports/college/2021/01/10/daughter-knows-best-holy-cross-womens-basketball-tops-army-again/6579197002/.

UC Berkley School of Information. "Jean Lave." California: UC Berkeley, n.d. Accessed February 15, 2022. http://lchcautobio.ucsd.edu/jean-lave/.

Voepel, Mechelle. "Holy Cross Routs Army as Coach Maureen Magarity Wins Clash with Dad." *ESPN.* January 9, 2021. https://www.espn.com/womens-college-basketball/story/_/id/30682392/holy-cross-routs-army-coach-maureen-magarity-wins-clash-dad.

CHAPTER 3

Hoebel, E. Adamson. *Anthropology: The Study of Man.* New York: McGraw Hill, 1972.

Bentz Høgseth, Harald. 2016. "Knowledge Transfer the Craftmen's Abstraction." In *Archaeology and Apprenticeship: Body Knowledge, Identity, and Communities of Practice,* 61–78. Arizona: The University of Arizona Press.

Janof, Tim. "Conversation with Bernard Greenhouse." *Cello-Bello.* August 11, 2016. https://www.cellobello.org/cello-blog/artistic-vision/conversation-with-bernard-greenhouse/.

Polanyi, Michael. *The Tacit Dimension.* Chicago: The University of Chicago Press, 2013.

CHAPTER 4

Acerbi, Alberto, Claudio Tennie, and Charles L. Nunn. "Modeling Imitation and Emulation in Constrained Search Spaces." *Learning & Behavior* 39, no. 2 (2010): 104–14. https://doi.org/10.3758/s13420-010-0009-z.

Cavalieri, Nate. "The Infamous Architecture of Chicago." *BBC.* August 2, 2010. https://www.bbc.com/travel/article/20100714-the-infamous-architecture-of-chicago.

Coles, William A., and Henry Hope Reed, eds. *Architecture in America: A Battle of Styles.* NY: Appleton-Century-Crofts, 1961.

Google. "To Ape—Google Search." *Google.* n.d. Accessed February 18, 2022. https://www.google.com/search?q=to+ape&rlz=1C1CHBF_enGH818GH818&oq=to+ape&aqs=chrome.69i57j0i512l2j0i10l2j0i512j0i10j69i60.1065j0j7&sourceid=chrome&ie=UTF-8.

History.com Editors. "Home Insurance Building." HISTORY. August 21, 2018. https://www.history.com/topics/landmarks/home-insurance-building.

Horner, Victoria, and Andrew Whiten. "Causal Knowledge and Imitation/Emulation Switching in Chimpanzees (Pan Troglodytes) and Children (Homo Sapiens)." *Animal Cognition* 8, no. 3 (2004): 164–81. https://doi.org/10.1007/s10071-004-0239-6.

Britannica. "Louis Sullivan—Legacy." *Encyclopedia Britannica,* n.d. Accessed February 28, 2021. https://www.britannica.com/biography/Louis-Sullivan/Legacy.

Manufacturing Intellect. "A Conversation with Frank Lloyd Wright (1953)." n.d. Video, 30:58. https://www.youtube.com/watch?v=W8EABJrMplY.

Nielsen, Mark, and Cornelia Blank. "Imitation in Young Children: When Who Gets Copied Is More Important than What Gets Copied." *Developmental Psychology* 47, no. 4 (2011): 1050–53. https://doi.org/10.1037/a0023866.

Tomasello, Michael. "Emulation Learning and Cultural Learning." *Behavioral and Brain Sciences* 21, no. 5 (1998): 703–4. https://doi.org/10.1017/s0140525x98441748. ————. "Culture and Cognitive Development." *Current Directions in Psychological Science* 9, no. 2 (2000): 37–40. https://doi.org/10.1111/1467-8721.00056.

twmanne. "Chimpanzee vs Human Child Learning (1_2).Flv." October 16, 2011. Video, 3:29. https://www.youtube.com/watch?v=JwwclyVYTkk.

Twombly, Robert. *Louis Sullivan, His Life and Work*. New York: Viking Penguin, 1986.

Wang, Z., R. A. Williamson, and A. N. Meltzoff. "Imitation as a Mechanism in Cognitive Development: A Cross-Cultural Investigation of 4-Year-Old Children's Rule Learning." *Frontiers of Psychology* (Original Research) (2015). https://doi.org/10.3389/fpsyg.2015.00562.

Whiten, A., and R. Ham. "On the Nature and Evolution of Imitation in the Animal Kingdom: Reappraisal of a Century of Research." *Advances in the Study of Behavior* 21 (1992): 239–83. DOI:10.1016/S0065-3454(08)60146-1.

Wood, Connor. 2020. "Why Imitation Is at the Heart of Being Human." *Greater Good*. January 23, 2020. https://greatergood.berkeley.edu/article/item/why_imitation_is_at_the_heart_of_being_human.

CHAPTER 5

Bandura, Albert. "Self-Efficacy: Toward a Unifying Theory of Behavioral Change." *Advances in Behaviour Research and Therapy* 1, no. 4 (1978): 139–61. https://doi.org/10.1016/0146-6402(78)90002-4. ————. 2012a. "ALBERT BANDURA Self Efficacy | Psychologist | Social Psychology | Stanford University | California." Albertbandura.com. 2012. https://albertbandura.com/albert-bandura-self-efficacy.html. Accessed February 22, 2022 ————. "On the Functional Properties of Perceived Self-Efficacy Revisited." *Journal of Management* 38, no. 1 (2012b): 9–44. https://doi.org/10.1177/0149206311410606.

Blamo Media. "Anchor—The Easiest Way to Make a Podcast." *Anchor*. July 15, 2020. https://anchor.fm/blamo-media/episodes/Jamie-Dimon---Chairman-and-CEO-of-JPMorgan-Chase-egn5as.

Dimon, Jamie. "Letter to Shareholders from Jamie Dimon, Annual Report 2020." *JPMorgan Chase & Co.* April 7, 2021. https://reports.jpmorganchase.com/investor-relations/2020/ar-ceo-letters.htm.

Langley, Monica. *Tearing Down the Walls: How Sandy Weill Fought His Way to the Top of the Financial World—and Then Nearly Lost It All.* New York: Free Press, 2004.

Locke, Taylor. "JPMorgan CEO Jamie Dimon on Being Fired: 'It Impacted My Net Worth, Not My Self Worth.'" *CNBC*. July 21, 2020. https://www.cnbc.com/2020/07/21/jpmorgan-ceo-jamie-dimon-on-being-fired.html.

McDonald, Duff. *Last Man Standing: The Ascent of Jamie Dimon and JPMorgan Chase*. London: Simon & Schuster, 2010.

CHAPTER 6

Barker, Andrew. "'Godfather of Black Music' Clarence Avant Looks Back." *Variety*. October 7, 2016. https://variety.com/2016/music/spotlight/clarence-avant-walk-of-fame-1201880651/.

Charles, Nick. "'Black Godfather': Netflix Documentary Profiles Clarence Avant, the Power Behind the Scenes." *NBC News*. January 7, 2020. https://www.nbcnews.com/news/nbcblk/black-godfather-netflix-documentary-profiles-clarence-avant-power-behind-scenes-n1103526.

Hart Research Associates. "Falling Short? College Learning and Career Success." American Association of Colleges and Universities, 2015. https://www.aacu.org/research/falling-short-college-learning-and-career-success.

Hodgson, Simon. "A Hell of a Businessman: A Biography of Joe Glaser." *Inside A.C.T,* January 29, 2016. http://blog.act-sf.org/2016/01/a-hell-of-businessman-biography-of-joe.html.

James, Frances. "The 21st Century Skills Gap: What Role Should Higher Education Institutions Play?" *QS*, February 15, 2021.

https://www.qs.com/the-21st-century-skills-gap-what-role-should-higher-education-institutions-play/.

Jones, Chris. "Behind a Great Trumpeter, the Notorious Joe Glaser." *Chicago Tribune*, January 29, 2016. https://www.chicagotribune.com/entertainment/theater/ct-armstrong-jones-ae-0131-20160128-column.html.

MOtvNetwork. "Clarence Avant & Quincy Jones—You'll Hit Something." Video, 1:05. December 8, 2011. https://www.youtube.com/watch?v=C71ZOOru58Q&list=PLB971A4E-A51648E51&index=13.

Netflix. 2019. "Watch the Black Godfather" Video, 1:57:59. May 20, 2019. https://www.netflix.com/watch/80173387?trackId=13752289&tctx=0%2C0%2Cf-b854a63ecd68453c4f3a859132d9e6aabe18882%3A4276a-9062631359de835c485787f94997b94dbf1%2Cfb854a-63ecd68453c4f3a859132d9e6aabe18882%3A4276a-9062631359de835c485787f94997b94dbf1%2Cun-known%2C%2C%2CtitlesResults.

Nilsson, Patricia. "What Top Employers Want from MBA Graduates." *Financial Times*, September 3, 2018. https://www.ft.com/content/64b19e8e-aaa5-11e8-89a1-e5de165fa619.

US Chamber of Commerce Foundation. *Hiring in the Modern Talent Marketplace*. US Chamber of Commerce Foundation, 2020. https://www.uschamberfoundation.org/reports/hiring-modern-talent-marketplace.

World Economic Forum. "The Future of Jobs Report 2020."
World Economic Forum, 2020. https://www.weforum.org/
reports/the-future-of-jobs-report-2020/digest.

CHAPTER 7

Clinton, Hillary Rodham. *Hard Choices: A Hillary Rodham
Clinton New Memoir.* New York: Simon & Schuster, 2014.

Eurich, Tasha. *Insight: The Surprising Truth About How Others
See Us, How We See Ourselves, and Why the Answers Matter
More Than We Think.* New York: Currency, 2018a. ———.
"The Right Way to Respond to Negative Feedback." *Harvard
Business Review*, May 31, 2018b. https://hbr.org/2018/05/the-
right-way-to-respond-to-negative-feedback.

Gallup. "How You Can Productively Aim Your Competition
Talents." *Gallup*, April 16, 2018. https://www.gallup.com/
cliftonstrengths/en/249857/competition-theme-productive-
ly-aim-your-cliftonstrengths-talent.aspx.

Rock, David, Beth Jones, and Chris Weller. "Using Neuroscience
to Make Feedback Work and Feel Better." *Strategy+Business*,
August 27, 2018. https://www.strategy-business.com/article/
Using-Neuroscience-to-Make-Feedback-Work-and-Feel-Bet-
ter.

CHAPTER 8

Greene, Robert. 2012. *Mastery.* New York: Penguin Books, 2012.

Hostin, Sunny, and Charisse Jones. *I Am These Truths: A Memoir of Identity, Justice, and Living between Worlds.* New York: Harperone, 2020.

Lufkin, Bryan. 2020. "How 'Reading the Air' Keeps Japan Running." *BBC,* January 30, 2020. https://www.bbc.com/worklife/article/20200129-what-is-reading-the-air-in-japan.

Meyer, Erin. "Navigating the Cultural Minefield." *Harvard Business Review.* May, 2014. https://hbr.org/2014/05/navigating-the-cultural-minefield.

Ng, Gorick. *The Unspoken Rules: Secrets to Starting Your Career off Right.* Boston, Massachusetts: Harvard Business Review Press, 2021. ———. "Gorick Ng's the Unspoken Rules." *Gorick,* 2022. https://www.gorick.com/.

The Wheel At TPH. "Watch the Replay of the Conversation Between Bishop T.D. Jakes & Pastor Joel Tudman Talk About Life, Generational Balance, and The Wheel. For..." *The Wheel at TPH,* December 10, 2021. Video, 4:02. https://www.facebook.com/watch/?v=639042510568085.

CHAPTER 9

AGOA.info. "AGOA Creates More than 300,000 Jobs in Africa." *Agoa.info,* n.d. https://agoa.info/news/article/4576-agoa-creates-more-than-300-000-jobs-in-africa.html.

The Economist. "The Heart of the Matter." *The Economist,* May 11, 2000. https://www.economist.com/special/2000/05/11/the-heart-of-the-matter.

CHAPTER 10

Bumiller, Elisabeth. "White House Letter: Politics and Prayer Mix in Post-Katrina Sermon." *The New York Times (World)*, September 19, 2005. https://www.nytimes.com/2005/09/19/world/americas/white-house-letter-politics-and-prayer-mix-in-postkatrina.html.

Gladwell, Malcolm. Outliers: The Story of Success. Boston, USA: Little, Brown and Company, 2008.

Greene, Robert. "The 3 Vital Steps of the Apprenticeship Phase." *HuffPost*, November 8, 2013. https://www.huffpost.com/entry/the-3-vital-steps-of-the-_b_4227085#:~:text=The%20Apprenticeship%20Phase%2D%2DThe%20Three%20Steps%20or%20Modes&text=These%20steps%20are%3A%20Deep%20Observation.

Jakes, T. D. "Transitions, Sonship, and Impartations with Bishop T.D. Jakes and Friends." Video, 1:26:47. January 20, 2022. https://www.youtube.com/watch?v=lzKKzjsFJXo.

Lave, J., and E. Wenger. *Situated Learning: Legitimate Peripheral Participation*. UK: Cambridge University Press, 1991. https://doi.org/10.1017/CBO9780511815355.